Called to Serve

THE MAKING OF A LADY LAWYER

Susan Walker Allen

Called to Serve

THE MAKING OF A LADY LAWYER

To the memory of my mother,
Marylou Neff Walker,
and my son, Kane Allen

"He will destroy death forever."

Isaiah 25:8

Contents

ACKNOWLEDGEMENTS

Love and thanks to Jim Moore, without whom this book would never have been finished.

Thanks to my legal colleagues for giving me so much grist for the writer's mill.

Grateful appreciation to all those who were excited to read my book.

Introduction by Dale W. Finley, Esq.

SUSAN WALKER ALLEN is a retired small-town attorney, and her memoir focuses on her experiences as she attempts to help her clients. I practiced law in the same town, under similar circumstances, and now realize that I knew less about her as a person than I thought.

Small-town attorneys often find themselves in strange situations, facing strange challenges. Attorneys in large law firms, corporations, and government agencies only concentrate on one or two legal specialties and never have to substitute as priests or inexpensive psychiatrists while struggling to understand their clients. Only small-town attorneys would be offered $50 to send postmortem letters to their client's children telling them where their mother's body might be found, and only *experienced* small-town attorneys would think fast enough to request another $2 for postage! Susan probably didn't have this particular experience, but small-town attorneys must specialize in whatever problems walk through their door.

Although attorneys often share their 'war stories' with other attorneys, they almost never write about them as Susan does. This has little to do with client confidentiality. Names have been changed and situations altered to protect the guilty and the occasional innocent. Additionally, the clients in these 'war stories' have often been deceased for a decade or more.

Susan writes the first such memoir I have read. She is a good writer, a good attorney, and a good person. She gives her readers insight into her experiences as a primarily solo practitioner of law, but there is much more to her book. The reader will quickly realize that Susan was determined to help her clients and, in the great majority of her cases, did just that. You may be surprised to learn that Susan valued a good result over a good fee. Making service a priority over money might seem a bit perverted to our fellow attorneys, but that is the way Susan's value system functions.

As you begin this book, you will see how daunting is the task of beginning a law practice alone. Law school graduates are typically sufficiently learned in the law, but completely inexperienced in the practical aspects of practice. Law schools don't really teach students how to present themselves to the public or how to make their case to a judge and jury. Once you're in solo practice, no one is sitting with you at the table passing notes. At the outset, you have no reputation for knowing or doing anything. If you are feeling secure and confident at this point, it is only because you do *not* know what you are doing.

There was, at the time Susan began her practice, another important factor. My artificial intelligence app tells me that during the fall semester of 2024 more than 56% of all law students in the United States were women, which is an increase of something like 2000% since Susan graduated in 1983. Anyway, the point is that she and the women who followed her needed real courage to open law offices and await the arrival of all the flotsam and jetsam that had been rejected by the more established attorneys. This is exactly what Susan Walker Allen did, and this book chronicles her early struggles.

Reading this book, you'll gain a unique perspective on the practice of law and the conduct of attorneys in general. Few of us view attorneys as they actually are, and many are surprised to discover that the majority of lawyers do not resemble anyone in their favorite television series. Readers will learn some rules of evidence, criminal procedure, various probate issues, basic guardianship considerations, adoption, divorce law, and assorted legal quirks. Most of this is incidental to the situations faced by Susan and her clients. While it's interesting information, it will likely not help you pass your bar exam. Susan's aim is to broaden your general understanding. You will also see how many of our 'domestic relations' laws have changed over the years as the position of women and the institution of marriage have evolved.

Susan has experienced the joy, redemption and inner satisfaction of having helped others get through their problems. Along the way, however, she suffered her own tragedy … one which can never be overcome via the sheer joy of a job well done. I won't elaborate on this point, because Susan has done an excellent job of conveying her unique circumstances and the heartbreak that followed.

Called to Serve is an engaging book—one that will almost certainly be read years from now as one of the few involving the practice of law by a woman during this period in our history. The book is informative and readable, and is made all the more important by the fact that readers will find nothing similar to it.

Dale W. Finley, Esq.
Russellville, Arkansas
Summer, 2025

CHAPTER ONE

Into the Maelstrom

In many ways, the last Saturday in June, 1978 was the last 'normal' day of my life. June 24 was the day before I left home to become a VISTA volunteer.

I remember my parents left early that morning to spend the weekend with relatives in another state. I would drive to Little Rock the following afternoon and fly to Texas to begin my VISTA orientation.

I was determined to make my life mean something to others. Over the past couple of weeks, I'd said goodbye to the things that had mattered most to me. Having graduated from Arkansas Tech University the month before, I'd put my postgraduate education on hiatus for a year to fulfill my commitment to VISTA. All of this was a dream in the making; I'd wanted to become a VISTA volunteer since I first read about the program in the eighth grade.

Quite often, making dreams come true requires a sacrifice. My boyfriend was devoted to me, but he was also a couple of years younger. I could hardly expect him to bide his time in Russellville while I spent a year in VISTA and then three years in law school out of state. One Friday evening in mid-June, I broke up with Jim.

Over the next couple of weeks, I spent free time with a few close friends. During the quiet nights and in those moments I could spend in search of myself, I tried to reframe my existence. Where once my thinking had been dominated by college courses and practice teaching, now I imagined coping with the challenge of living on a small VISTA stipend while I found a way to make a difference in the world.

The VISTA program was born of John Kennedy's dreams and Lyndon Johnson's domestic agenda, and by the time I joined in the late 1970s, it already had something of a checkered past. Since 1965, young Americans like me had joined the fight against poverty, working toward the goal of the 'great society' that liberal social engineers still held was possible.

VISTA volunteers have served in all 50 states and in all United States territories, helping local organizations expand their capacity to engineer change. Today, VISTA workers serve largely in office settings, work that prepares them for a career in the public, private or nonprofit sectors. Back in my day, however, VISTA assignments and neighborhood involvement were a little more hands-on. While I've never been afraid to get my hands dirty, I was completely unprepared for the inner-city poverty, crime and turmoil I'd be confronting.

All that lay ahead of me on that beautiful Saturday in late June, 1978. I spent the day deciding what to take with me and what to leave behind. I was walking away from one world and rushing headlong into another. I felt the freedom and exhilaration one often feels at the start of a long journey.

The only difference was that the journey on which I was embarking had an uncertain outcome. That evening, I fell into my mother's bed and discovered that I was too excited to sleep.

Tomorrow, I thought, *I'll begin to set the world right.*

I credit my sweet mother with instilling in me early on the idea that I had a responsibility to serve others. My mother was Marylou Neff Walker, one of the most Christlike people I have ever known. Mother was born in Indiana and raised by a Brethren minister. My grandparents on both sides were stern, austere people, as Hoosiers tended to be back then. In sharp contrast to her upbringing, my mother brought life, joy and happiness everywhere she went. In all the ways that mattered, my mother was my best inspiration.

I was born in Aurora, Colorado, a Denver suburb. The year was 1956. I have an older sister, Elizabeth. My father, Kenneth Roland Walker, was teaching history at the Air Force Academy in Aurora. Daddy had already earned his doctorate in history; he eventually received a Master's in Political Science. Rather than continue to move us around like a military family, daddy left the Air Force, joined the Air Force Reserves and moved us to Russellville, Arkansas when I was two years old. My father taught history and political science at Arkansas Tech University for 40 years. In the early 1990s, daddy took a year off from teaching to write *A History of Arkansas Tech University.* The history of Tech was his third book. His first, published when I was about 10 years old, was *The Days the Presidents Died.* In the 1970s, daddy finished *A History of the Middle West.*

Once we'd settled in Russellville, my family attended the First United Methodist church. Daddy sang in the church choir; my mother taught sixth grade Sunday School for over 20 years. By the time I was finishing elementary school, I knew that if I did not help others and love my neighbor as myself, I would be a failure as a human being. My mother stayed home with me until I was in third grade. Then she went back to work as a reading teacher at Crawford Elementary school. When I was in sixth grade, mother went to the new Sequoyah Elementary school on the south side of Russellville and started the school library. She was the librarian at Sequoyah for nearly 20 years before she retired in 1985.

When I was in ninth grade, I read *Clarence Darrow for the Defense* by Irving Stone. The book inspired me to become an attorney. Two years later, during my junior year in high school, I decided to shadow a local attorney to see what being a lawyer was really like. I talked with Mr. Billings, my counselor, and he arranged for me to spend a day shadowing Jon Sanford. I remember I was shaky with anticipation. Jon was cordial. In his office, he essentially told me that life as an attorney was mighty dull. “You have to write, read and research most of the time,” he said.

Jon also mentioned that attorneys need to spend a good deal of time listening to clients. As if on cue, a client appeared in his office and Jon asked me to wait outside. I gathered I’d have to content myself with the outdated magazines in Jon’s waiting room. Jon’s partner, Jim Pate, breezed in an hour late. He towered over me as he shook my hand, then he went straight to his office and closed the door. I was left to cool my heels.

At lunchtime, Jon emerged from his office. “See you after lunch,” he said. I walked—alone—to a local drug store and had a salad and ice cream at their little soda fountain. Then I returned to Jon’s office and spent the remainder of the afternoon sitting in the lobby.

That little ‘shadowing’ exercise made me realize that a female attorney just wasn’t wanted, at least not by the all-male Russellville legal conclave. I imagine Jon and Jim thought that a day spent in quiet contemplation would make me reconsider a future in law. In fact, it did exactly the opposite.

I graduated fourth in my class at Russellville High School, then earned my Bachelor’s in Elementary Education at Arkansas Tech. By the time I was finishing high school, I knew I wanted to be a VISTA volunteer. At that point, I thought I wanted to serve in South America. In the late 1970s, however, there was ongoing civil unrest in that part of the hemisphere, so I opted to remain in the United States. That was probably a wise decision; I was a naive girl who had never been alone and far from home.

When I left Russellville, I thought I was going to Houston. I flew first to Dallas, Texas. During the week of initial volunteer training, my assignment changed: I would stay in Dallas. What did I know about Houston? Not much. At that time, Houston was the largest city in the United States with no effective zoning. I can’t say that staying in Dallas was a relief, exactly, but I was determined to do what good I could wherever I could.

I moved my suitcases into a small, furnished one-bedroom apartment in a shabby Oak Cliff complex on East Ninth Street. With no automobile or even a bicycle, my usual mode of transport was the city bus.

Growing up in Arkansas, I had been a part of a comfortable majority. Most of the people I saw and interacted with were white and middle-class like me. In the Oak Cliff suburb, on the other hand, I was a distinct minority. I was often the only caucasian on the city bus. The move from usual and customary to unwelcome outsider took me by complete surprise.

I soon realized that, like most VISTA volunteers, I had no real power to effect change. Our tasks were to lobby for better roads, help build community parks and improve drainage in struggling neighborhoods. I was also assigned to be a tutor in a West Dallas housing project school, serving the poorest children in the poorest part of the city. I took public transportation everywhere I went. Getting off the bus was an adventure; waiting for it was the scariest time of my life. I didn't know whether I would be mugged, raped or both.

As it happened, I was nearly raped twice. As a VISTA newcomer, I had nothing to do over the July 4 holiday. I went down to the street corner to catch a city bus, not knowing that the buses weren't running on the holiday. July 4 was a very warm day, as Independence Day tends to be in Texas. I remember I was standing on the sidewalk; the sun was hot and growing hotter. A Hispanic man stopped and asked if I needed help. I told him I was waiting on the bus.

"The buses aren't running today," he told me.

I wanted to go do some girl shopping downtown, which was a three- or four-minute drive via the freeways. In Dallas, however, the expressways were very busy and walking was quite unsafe. I got into the man's car, and he looked at me.

He certainly didn't seem dangerous; as I remember, he was a little overweight but had a nice smile.

The man drove me onto Stemmons Freeway and past downtown Dallas. I could see the West End quite clearly as that part of the city slid past. I asked him where he was going; he said he was just taking me for a drive. After about 20 minutes, my chauffeur stopped at an isolated park alongside the Trinity riverbed. He told me to get out of the car.

This was noontime in Dallas, and not a creature was stirring. I did not feel danger, but my antenna were up. The man walked me over to a secluded tree, proceeded to pin me to the ground, then tried to kiss and make out with me.

I told him 'No' very firmly, but he didn't seem to hear and kept groping me.

I finally realized I was in danger and slapped him hard across the face. "No!" I screamed.

Aside from my would-be rapist, my other immediate problem was lack of transportation. The man could well leave me alone and lost in a deserted city park. Since I had just slapped him—the only time I've ever really slapped someone in my entire life—he seemed likely to do just that.

Finally, he held up his hands and offered me a ride back to downtown. When he stopped on Main Street, I got out of his car without looking back.

I eventually learned to go to my assignments with another VISTA volunteer, but absorbing that lesson took time. Meanwhile, I had another close call. One fall day, after I had finished tutoring, I went out to catch the bus to my apartment in Oak Cliff. Unfortunately, the bus took some time to get there; in the black neighborhoods, Dallas buses didn't run on schedule.

While I was waiting, a somewhat older black man approached me.

"Hey, Honey! You sure are beautiful. What are you doing in this part of town?"

I told him I'd just finished tutoring and was returning to my apartment.

"No, you're not," he said. "You're coming with me." He grabbed me and pulled me toward him; I fought him. Just then, the bus came and I broke free and ran to it. I never saw the man again, and I never tutored in the West Dallas housing project again.

The summer of 1978 and the ensuing winter were among the hottest and coldest in recent history. Our 'block partnership' finally assumed traction late in the summer, and I seized the opportunity to team up with other VISTA volunteers. Lynn Klein, a redheaded Jewish girl, took to riding the city bus with me. Lynn was more exotic than pretty, in a Barbra Streisand sort of way. Our community organizer, Roz, got things done by ignoring all the rules. Roz was a small black woman with an Afro; she'd have us all over for block parties in her apartment. I would often take refuge there that winter, when I had no heat at home.

I did have a roof over my head, but it wasn't much. VISTA paid $255 per month, and I got about $80 worth of food stamps. I still remember the hostile looks I got when I pulled out food stamps at the local supermarket. My apartment rent was about $150 a month, which left me with very little spending money. My mother and other relatives sent me cash from time to time, so I managed to scrape by.

At some point during my first few months in Dallas, I came to the realization that in order for people to pay attention to me, I'd need a law degree. I was just a thin young woman with a soft voice. I could change the world, but I required more tools than I had at that point.

When I went home for Christmas, I began applying to law schools. I knew I wanted to focus on consumer and environmental law, so I looked toward law schools that would help me focus on those fields of study. To pacify my parsimonious father, I applied to both the University of Arkansas at Fayetteville and UA Little Rock law schools, but I also applied to Emory University in Atlanta and the University of San Diego. I'd fallen in love with that part of southern California during a trip with daddy some years before, and I remembered San Diego with great fondness.

Deep down, I was hoping to be admitted to the University of San Diego because I loved the San Diego Zoo … in my opinion, the best zoo in the United States. I had also enjoyed the beautiful beaches and the rather exotic Old Town. Perhaps more importantly, USD also had an amazing consumer law department. Dr. Robert Fellmeth had been a 'Nader's Raider,' and the Center for Public Interest Law was well-established by the time I entered law school.

That spring, I got acceptance letters from all four law schools. Deciding to go to San Diego required no deliberation and no real exercise of intellect. Even though I knew student loans would be necessary if I wanted to attend law school there, the University of San Diego was my first choice. USD is a private Catholic university; the law school was founded in 1954 and is usually ranked in the top 100 law schools in the United States. The campus covers about 180 acres and is dotted with 16th-century Renaissance-style buildings. Of course, southern California weather is little short of idyllic, and I looked forward to that. I'd had enough of freezing winters and the Dallas noonday sun.

Somehow, I made it through the balance of my VISTA year. I finally came back to Arkansas in late June, 1979. My boyfriend—the same long-suffering guy to whom I'd said farewell a year before—picked me up at the airport and did his best to help me enjoy the rest of the summer. Then I picked a fight with Jim a couple of weeks before I headed off to law school and we broke up again.

I was lucky enough to win a USD lottery for a student apartment, one of about six the University had available. The fact that this was *my* apartment meant I could pick and choose my roommates, and shuffling roommates would become something of a necessity in the years to come.

I flew to San Diego and found the USD campus as sunny and inviting as the catalog photos had foretold. My apartment was on Goshen Street—a small coincidence, since my parents hailed from Goshen, Indiana—and the university was a short hike up the hill. I loved the sparkling white adobe architecture of the campus buildings. I settled into the class routine fairly quickly, found a study equilibrium that worked for me, and generally enjoyed my first semester. The work I did during those first months would count for a third of my first-year grade; the second semester would count for two-thirds.

During those first few weeks in law school, I felt like I was watching a foreign film without subtitles. Law lingo was commonplace in the classroom, and I didn't know much. I had to learn what a contract was. I thought a tort was something one ate. Suffice it to say it took me time to catch on to what the instructors and students were discussing. The weighty Black's Law Dictionary became a constant companion.

I made it through the first semester exams, spent the holiday season at home with my parents and then returned to California. I got back to the daily grind in mid-January. Then, on Valentine's evening, I was walking down the hall in my apartment and passed out.

I came around soon enough, picked myself up and went back to bed. I went to class as usual the next morning. I remember that was a Friday, and I was looking forward to the weekend so I could recuperate. That afternoon, I felt sick to my stomach, and then the pain became unbearable. The campus physician sent me to the emergency room. Since I had no car and could not ride my moped, I had to take a cab.

At nearby Mercy hospital, the attending physician diagnosed appendicitis and told me I needed immediate surgery. I was in the hospital for six days; my mother flew out to be with me, which I appreciated very much. Unfortunately, the ER doctor's diagnosis was incorrect; after the surgeon made a wide incision, he discovered that my appendix was only 'slightly inflamed.' I suffer from renal fusion, or 'horseshoe kidney.' My kidneys are joined together, forming a shape like a horseshoe. This is a congenital condition, affecting about 1 in 500 people.

I had a raging kidney infection which, for someone with only one large kidney, was quite serious. When I went home from the hospital, I thought I could be up and back in class in a few days. But as my incision slowly healed, just climbing the San Diego hills was agony. My classmates recorded lectures and brought the tapes to me, but I fell further and further behind ... not a good thing for a first-year law student.

I eventually decided to withdraw from classes and retake the first year of law school. After about six weeks' rest in my apartment, I went out to look for a job. I became a food server in a nursing home, working for minimum wage. I was setting out meals for the residents. That was a soul-crushing experience; thankfully, it lasted only two weeks.

I'd also applied to be a server—in '80s parlance, a waitress—at a local Bob's Big Boy restaurant. I got that job and left the nursing home behind. Over the next four months before I started back to school, I made the minimum wage salary but great tips. Suffice it to say I was a very good waitress! The customers seemed to like me, I had a good memory and a cheery disposition, and I didn't mind the hours. I did gain some weight, however; the readily available hot fudge and ice cream proved too tempting to resist.

My mother came to San Diego to spend a couple of weeks while I was still working at Bob's. She would head down to the beach in the mornings and enjoy the surf while I was still asleep. My typical workday ended in the early morning hours.

I reentered law school late that summer, enduring the scathing looks that befit someone coming back to repeat her freshman year. That fall, when the pressure grew unbearable, I retreated to my bedroom and re-read the card my mother had sent me when I first got to San Diego:

Hold fast to dreams,
for if dreams die,
life is a broken-winged bird
that cannot fly.

My dream was to become an honest lawyer and change the world one client at a time. My mother's encouragement notwithstanding, I came to the realization that changing the world might require more than a law degree. There's a reason why many people hate attorneys.

Committed, I soldiered on. I successfully completed my first year—again—and then my second and third years in law school flashed by. In my second year, I signed up as a student in the Consumer Protection Clinic. Each student was assigned to a couple of State boards or commissions. I was appointed to monitor the California Architects Board and the Guide Dogs for the Blind. When either board had a public meeting, I would attend the gathering and then write a synopsis of their discussion. These summaries were compiled into the quarterly publication of the Center for Public Interest Law.

If an agency or board was obviously unnecessary or accomplishing nothing, the Center would focus on trying to dissolve that board or commission. Some State boards were legitimately needed. For example, the Board of Cosmetology regulated the licensing of cosmetologists and had to ensure that a cosmetology student passed relevant coursework and tests before becoming a beautician.

For two years in law school, I was also one of the Center's student workers. My job included monitoring the Sierra Club, World Wildlife Fund, Natural Resource Defense Council and other non-profit environmental groups. I would condense the group's accomplishments into an article for the Center's quarterly publication.

I enjoyed working for the Center and liked being with like-minded students and staff who cared about advancing consumer and environmental law. However, I wasn't the same exceptional student I'd been back in Arkansas; there were too many brilliant minds and too much content to absorb. By the time I graduated, in May, 1983, I was already gearing up to take the California Bar.

Saying that the California Bar exam is difficult would be an understatement. The California Bar is considered one of the most challenging exams of its kind in the United States, primarily due to low historical pass rates. For example, of the 4,205 applicants who took the Bar in early 2020, only 1,128 passed—an overall pass rate of less than 27%. Interestingly, first-time applicants tend to fare better than repeat applicants. About 40% of first-timers pass, while only about 22% of repeaters succeed.

I was studying to take the Bar when something impelled me to reach out to Jim, my former boyfriend in Russellville. At that point, Jim was pursuing a corporate archivist position with Wrather Corporation, and he was planning to fly to California a few weeks later. At the time, Wrather owned the Queen Mary, the famous floating hotel in Long Beach. Jim interviewed onboard the ship one Friday, then drove to San Diego to see me the next day. We had a wonderful weekend and essentially picked up where we'd left off four years before. We even drove back up to Long Beach and had a nice lunch on the grand old Queen Mary. We also saw Howard Hughes' Spruce Goose, which was displayed under a massive dome in the same beachside development.

I took the California bar in late July. After a three-day torture session, I felt certain I had failed. I heard nothing from the state for the next five months. Finally, on December 31, I received a notice that I'd passed. However, I never practiced law in California. I had returned to Arkansas in early August, 1983.

You might think the shift in geography an odd decision. I'd certainly become accustomed to living in paradise, but I suppose I missed my home. I'd already found that I didn't enjoy the big city. On a trip to the San Francisco area for a law conference, I'd seen firsthand the same sort of open poverty and suffering I'd battled as a VISTA volunteer. After four years in San Diego, I'd had enough. I gave up my little apartment with a song of thanksgiving on my lips, packed my suitcases and went back home.

Any notion that I was the prodigal daughter was quickly dispelled when I arrived back home; my parents simply treated me as if I'd never left. While I enjoyed the peace and quiet of life in the country and reveled in the sheer comfort of being back home again, I also needed a little more freedom than my parents were accustomed to providing me. The fact that I was 26 years old didn't enter into the equation, nor did the fact that I was now a Juris Doctor. I hadn't yet taken the Arkansas Bar and had no income of my own. I might as well have been back in junior high.

Jim had a small apartment a couple of miles from my parents' house, and I spent a good deal of time with him that summer. By then, Jim was the *de facto* manager of a couple of local radio stations, and he was gone from very early in the morning until late afternoon. I soaked up the tranquility like a sponge, enjoying the apartment complex swimming pool and my early evening rendezvous with Jim. Jim's apartment became a sanctuary … a sort of home away from home, and I was grateful for it.

Jim didn't get the job with Wrather Corporation. Having essentially grown up in broadcasting, Jim had long realized that if he stayed in radio, he would be penniless and an old man by the time he was 50. Unfortunately, there were few business opportunities in Russellville that were suited to an up-and-coming guy like him. A few weeks after I returned to Arkansas, Jim made the rather painful decision to leave me and leave the state, embarking on a 25-year career with Success Motivation International, which was headquartered in Texas. Jim parlayed his public speaking ability into sales success and became one of that company's brightest stars, earning SMI's Rookie of the Year award for 1984 and then serving as executive director, communications director and corporate archivist. Along the way, he began writing books. His book on the Kennedy assassination, *Conspiracy of One,* was published in 1990, and Jim signed a copy to me when he returned to Russellville to promote another book in late 1993.

I wasn't bereft without Jim, certainly, but I missed his company. A good friend suggested I go meet a new chemistry professor at Arkansas Tech, Dr. Bob Allen. Bob, my friend told me, was a staunch advocate of a nuclear 'freeze' and had enlisted other professors and students at Arkansas Tech in a crusade against the arms race. As a result, professors were proselytizing students on a daily basis in the Tech classrooms.

I drove to Tech, walked into McEver Hall, and found Bob's office. Bob was there. He was tall, with wire-rimmed glasses like John Lennon's. He had twinkling blue eyes like my mother. He had a striped multicolored sweater that cheered me immensely. For whatever reason, I knew instantly that Bob was a good person.

Bob was a decade older than me, but in many ways, we were kindred spirits. Bob had actively protested the Vietnam war and was at the May, 1970 general strike protest on the University of Oklahoma campus. He received a draft deferment because of his persistent migraines. I like to think that the draft board knew Bob was trouble from the start.

Bob had earned a Bachelor's degree in organic chemistry from the University of Oklahoma in 1969. Five years later, Bob completed his doctorate in organic chemistry at OU. He dedicated his dissertation to the victims of the Kent State massacre and to all the young Americans who had fallen in Vietnam. Degree in hand, Bob headed north. He finished his post-doctoral fellowship at Dartmouth College in New Hampshire, then began teaching at

Sangamon State University in Springfield, Illinois. Dr. Allen came to Arkansas Tech in 1981.

For about an hour that afternoon, I sat with Bob and talked. In many ways, I came to believe that Bob was the 'Mr. Berkeley' for whom I'd searched in vain during my time in California. Before I left, I asked Bob out on a date. He accepted. I cooked a picnic-style dinner and we drove to his home in the country and had a quiet evening.

Bob drove a bright orange Datsun pickup truck. Back then, orange was an unusual color for an automobile; I thought it an omen because Jim had an orange Chevrolet. On my third date with Bob, we went for a hike through the Ozark Highlands trail. The early December day was chilly but not cold. After a long walk, we came back exhausted.

Up to that point, Bob hadn't touched me at all. I remember we were driving back along scenic Highway 7. I turned to Bob, who was driving, and asked, "Are you gay? You haven't tried to kiss me."

Bob laughed. "I definitely want to kiss you," he finally replied. When we got back to his mobile home, he did.

Jim drove from Texas to spend a Saturday night with me just before Christmas, 1983. I think it was obvious to both of us that our romance had run its course. Jim was as devoted and attentive as ever, but he seemed myopically focused on the success courses he was selling. All in all, I found Jim had become a little too much like daddy. That made sense; my father had been Jim's college advisor and something of a mentor. Jim and I spent the night together in Little Rock and parted as friends the next day, but only after I told him that I'd met Bob and felt certain that Bob and I would wind up together. I remember being both sad and excited that Yuletide. The sense of loss was pervasive, but the excitement I felt at the start of a long journey was back full force.

Things happened as I foretold them. Bob's laidback, backwoods lifestyle and amazing intellect proved too much for me to resist, and we were married in May, 1985. Ours was a partnership that stood the test of time; we were still happily together when Bob passed away in 2021. Our only child, Kane, was just 17 when he was killed in an automobile accident in early 2007. I'll share that story later in this book.

Of course, all of that lay far ahead of me as I became a member of the Bar in 1984. Suffice it to say that I never dreamed I'd be swept into the maelstrom of a law career in quite the way I was.

CHAPTER TWO

Lady Lawyer

EVEN AFTER SPENDING 36 YEARS PRACTICING LAW, I never became accustomed to being called a "lady lawyer." I often replied that I was only a lawyer. I was a lawyer first and foremost. However, there was no getting around the fact that I was the first female attorney in our five-county region. I started my practice in 1984 and remained the only local 'lady lawyer' for about four years before another female attorney began handling cases in Pope County.

When I moved out of my San Diego apartment in early August, 1983, I was almost certain I had failed the California Bar examination. Once I was back in Arkansas, I told my boyfriend that I was 95 percent sure I'd failed. Through the summer and into the fall, there was no word; typically, Bar exams take some time to grade. I spent Christmas with my parents and I was at their home on New Year's Eve day when I finally received a letter from San Francisco.

I took my time opening the envelope, because I just *knew* the result would not be to my liking. I unfolded the letter and read:

Dear Counselor:
Welcome to the State Bar of California.

To gain admission to the Bar, you have demonstrated the highest professional standards in our nation. You passed one of the most stringent ethics tests, and members have taken the oath to uphold the U. S. Constitution ...

I can recall only a few moments in my life when I was more ecstatic than that afternoon! After the four years of hell that were my law school experience, I'd finally become an attorney. I could begin planning my career with something I had not possessed until that New Year's Eve: The conviction that I could actually *practice* law.

In early January, 1984, Chancery Court Judge Richard Mobley administered the oath that officially made me a member of the Bar. Judge Mobley was a good family friend and a fine man; the next year, he officiated at my wedding. But I'm getting ahead of myself.

Not long after the turn of the year, I realized I was already in love with Professor Allen. Bob loved me, I was certain, but he was also in love with the oak-filled woods, where he lived, and Arkansas Tech, where he taught. I knew that if I was going to be with Bob, I would have to stay in Arkansas and practice law in Russellville. Over the past summer and fall, I'd found myself settling back into the quiet, calm country life I'd so enjoyed while I was growing up. The prospect of spending my career in my home state did not seem as oppressive as it had when I was in VISTA or in law school.

I spent a good deal of time with Bob after the holidays while I studied for the Arkansas Bar. Of course, we were both testing our relationship and watching how we interacted. I took the Arkansas Bar exam at the end of February, 1984. I looked forward to taking another Bar exam about as much as I'd have looked forward to a root canal, but the test was a necessary step if I intended to stay with Bob and practice in my home state.

In comparison to the California Bar, the Arkansas exam was a piece of cake. I'd already passed the California Bar and did not have to take the multi-state portion again. I became licensed to practice in Arkansas at the end of the March. I moved to Little Rock and started working at the Prosecutor Coordinator's Office on April 1.

Bob and his two teenaged sons would come to pick me up on Friday afternoons and we'd spend the weekends on Bob's hardscrabble farm north of Dover.

I finally left the Little Rock job and came home for good in mid-August, 1984, and I hung out my shingle in Russellville. Law school might have taught me the law, but it had done nothing to prepare me for the challenge of running my own business, and entrepreneurship did not come naturally to me. As strange as it sounds, our law school professors had never really reviewed legal documents, and I had to find templates for those I would need most often. I remember the first time I actually had the opportunity to read a decree of divorce! Some of my male contemporaries helped me develop the legal document frameworks I would use for decades.

Somehow, I muddled through the first couple of years. I managed to break the 'glass ceiling' of the Pope County courthouse as a trial attorney. By 1985, I'd won my first trial in a Russellville courtroom. Convinced that I might enjoy even greater success if I partnered with another local attorney, I entered into the first of two partnerships. The first firm was Shermer and Walker; since I was just a female lawyer, I got second billing. I had decided to keep my maiden name for the time being, and I practiced as 'M. Susan Walker.' The 'M.' was for Mary, my first name that had gone largely unused since my mother's colleagues called her 'Mary.' I had grown up in Russellville and fancied myself moderately well-known; I thought keeping 'Walker' might be something of a slight edge.

A couple of years later, my friend David Gibbons, who was working with our Municipal Judge, Richard Peel, decided to leave Peel's practice and move into his own office. David and I had become friends because we were both defending criminal clients. In early 1988, I sat up shop with David.

By the time I went into partnership with David Gibbons, I'd been married for nearly three years. In May, 1985, Bob Allen and I said our vows in my parents' crowded living room. We had a brief honeymoon and visited relatives across the Midwest, then I went back to the law office in Russellville and Bob returned to teaching at Arkansas Tech. We finished building Bob's dream home on about 18 acres in the rural edge of northern Pope County, and I settled into the life of a small-town attorney who spent her nights and weekends miles away from the office, deep in the forests of northwest Arkansas. That wonderful normalcy lasted for about three years.

I came to view Bob as something of a Renaissance man, but if he was any one thing, he was an environmentalist. Bob was deeply concerned about the future of the earth and determined to leave as small a carbon footprint as possible. We built our home to take advantage of the sun's heat, and we had a central wood-burning stove to take the chill off winter evenings. We recycled paper and cardboard, cans, plastic and glass. Bob even eschewed our propane-powered clothes dryer; I became accustomed to hanging our clothes out to dry outside. In wintertime, I used an indoor clothesline that stretched across the two- story atrium that was our living room.

Whenever we could, we were outside hiking or canoeing, enjoying the tranquility and abundant wildlife and finding our way as a couple. Marriage is an adjustment, and the solitude of our home helped us feel comfortable with each other.

Bob was an expert in most areas of physical science, and an adept student of the political scene. His long unkempt hair and beard meant that many people around these parts discounted him, which was a monumental mistake. Beneath that hippie-ish exterior lay an extraordinary intellect. Bob converted several conventionally powered vehicles to run on biodiesel fuel made from discarded restaurant waste oil. At one point, he powered an older Mercedes Benz sedan with waste oil and drove the vehicle back and forth to his classes at Arkansas Tech. Bob even began teaching the biodiesel conversion process to other locals.

Over nearly 36 years of our marriage, Bob became something of a professional contrarian. I cannot make much sense of life without religion, but Bob felt that religion defied science or any attempt at rational explanation. He wrote newspaper editorials that reflected his liberal bias. Once our son Kane was in school, I ran for judge. I found that Bob's out-of-the-box thinking had effectively poisoned the political well for me. Many of my colleagues would not vote for me because they found my husband's political and religious views untenable.

Bob was the long-term president of the Piney Creek chapter of the Arkansas Canoe Club. In the spring, he'd teach water safety and navigation concepts to each new canoe school group. I became accustomed to helping Bob host Canoe Club Christmas parties and other river gatherings, and Bob's compatriots became an important social outlet for both of us over the years.

My mother had decided to retire from teaching about the time Bob and I were married. Mother was looking forward to traveling to see relatives and spending time sewing, painting and pursuing various hobbies. Within a couple of months of her retirement, however, she was being plagued by increasingly severe headaches. That fall, she was diagnosed with aggressive brain cancer. The extended nursing home stay that followed was a nightmare for my father, my sister and me. My long-suffering mother died on December 18, 1987. Her memorial service in early 1988 was full to overflowing; even Jim, my former boyfriend, flew from Texas to attend. Everyone had a story to tell about how mother had touched their life in one way or another. Mother was a saint, and I remember being struck that winter by the sort of example she'd set. I had a lot to live up to.

Our little community was reeling from losses that Christmas. Broomfield Road, about five miles east of where Bob and I lived, became the scene of the worst family mass murder in United States history. Not content to have killed more than a dozen members of his immediate family, Gene Simmons drove into Russellville and shot four others. Two of his victims died instantly; one was Richard Peel's secretary. Like many other local attorneys, I spent the day with my office doors bolted and locked. Two of my local law colleagues were eventually appointed to defend Simmons, and his lunacy plagued Pope County until he was executed in the summer of 1990.

Mother had been dead just a year when I became pregnant. At that point, I was feeling her loss quite keenly; I would have treasured her help and guidance. Why? Because I was the first lady lawyer in the area, I discovered that being pregnant was something of an ordeal. My partner knew since the inception of our partnership early that same year that I wanted to have a baby. "No problem," David said at the time.

By May, 1989, my pregnancy was becoming rather evident. Two divorce clients summarily fired me and hired another attorney because they thought I might not come back to the office after I had the baby. Despite my assurances that I would only be on maternity leave for a couple of months and that David could handle their cases in my absence, I still got the boot.

Our son, Nickolas Kane Allen was born on September 20. I'd babysat rather a lot while I was in high school and college and I'd cared for my sister's little boys periodically, so I was well-prepared to deal with a newborn. Determined to breastfeed, I stayed at home with Kane for the first six weeks. Our life in the country and our determination to recycle provided some unforeseen challenges; I was up at all hours of the night, nursing Kane. I often thought that Kane's crying must have stirred the forest animals from their nests! Our living room clothesline was festooned with the baby's cloth diapers and plastic pants.

I remember being extraordinarily sleep-deprived. The baby nursed every hour or so at first, even in the middle of the night, so a solid evening's sleep became a thing of the past for a year or so. As Kane grew, the nursing intervals decreased a bit, but I was still up and feeding the baby every couple of hours. Those first several months were a fitful time for Bob and me. To this day, I don't know how I made it through ... especially driving to Russellville and back each day, which was a 40-mile commute.

Despite some ear infections, Kane thrived. Making the transition from home care to daycare was not without challenges. When I returned to work in early November, I was still expressing my breastmilk at regular intervals during the day. After taking Kane to his daycare, I would go to my office in the mornings and struggle to stay awake. I remember that my midday office meal was typically a brown bag lunch while I was attached to my breast pump. Kane spent his days in a local daycare, I knew the owners and I was certain they would lavish attention on my baby.

The little 30-minute breastmilk pumping sessions threatened to overfill our office refrigerator with small bottles of light blue milk. Although it's hard to imagine how he might have mistaken my breastmilk for creamer, my law partner poured some into his coffee. I didn't know this had happened until three years after the fact, and when I found out, I was flabbergasted.

I'd been back at work only a few days when another male colleague told me that I should be at home with my baby boy rather than working. His wife did not work outside the home, and had borne him five children. She even washed his car, something he often reported to me with pride. How I wished I had a spouse who would wash my car and cook for me! Someone who could handle laundry would have been greatly appreciated.

David Gibbons, my law partner, protested that I was taking too much time to raise my son and derided my husband for not doing more to help with the baby. Kane was less than a year old; there was little more Bob might have done. Finally, David decided my 'divided loyalties' were too much for him to handle, and he ended our partnership in June, 1990. Unfortunately, David had no credit and our building lease was in my name. When I pointed to the lease I signed, David became a bit aggressive.

"Don't try to start a fight with me," he told me sternly, as if my being the signatory on the office lease was a matter of no importance.

"Just be sure to pay the rent," I replied. I note this sort of dismissal with some degree of pride; I was not as cynical or paranoid back then.

Bob helped me move out of the office one Friday afternoon, and I moved into a small suite in Russellville's One Main Place the following week. The title sounds far more grand than the actual location; One Main Place was a huge, flat building with small offices and no conference room. I had two offices and a main reception area, along with a small office for my secretary. How I managed to practice there for a decade amazes me nowadays, but I was quite successful. In 2000, I bought a small house a couple of blocks away and converted the former residence into an office. Then, in 2006, I bought a large, 100-year-old two-story house which became my office until I retired in the spring of 2020.

Once I was happily ensconced in the minuscule space that was One Main Place, I changed my name, adding "Allen" to the masthead, and I've been known for the past 30-odd years as Susan Walker Allen. The change came at a prudent time, and I would not have wanted to have Kane grow up with folks thinking he'd come from a broken home.

When you are actively involved in any profession for decades on end, you meet some interesting folks along the way. Mary Bhardwaj worked with me for a year or two in the mid or late 1990s; Mary was my partner, but she would never take any pay. She didn't need the money. She and Vas, her husband, had been my sponsors when

I joined Russellville's Central Presbyterian Church. Mary and Vas had a daughter a few weeks before my son was born, so she and I were kindred spirits of a sort. Mary and Vas moved out of state in the late 1990s when Vas' engineering work required the move. In many respects, Mary was the best partner I ever had.

From the beginning of my practice, I veered toward a specialization in family law. A female attorney was generally sought after for divorces and family matters. As a result, I handled custody fights, child support, visitation disputes and even probate of wills.

I'd considered real estate law, but one land dispute cured me of that desire forever. I also dabbled in unemployment cases, but wound up litigating or settling very few. Instead, I focused on workers' compensation cases, and I helped many local residents who were disabled or injured at work obtain Social Security payments. These cases were heard before an Administrative Law Judge; there was no opposing counsel. All I had to do was argue the case before a judge, and quite often, even that effort was not required. Many Social Security applicants were approved without a hearing.

By the time my partnership with David Gibbons had run its course, serving children and the disenfranchised poor had become my priority. I worked through a number of guardianship cases with a view toward keeping children out of foster care and away from the Department of Human Services. As you might expect, I found the child abuse and neglect cases astonishingly depressing. I was able to fall back on my teacher training; even before I had my son, I knew the sort of care and nutrition a baby or child required. I was able to recognize signs of neglect that most practitioners wouldn't have found evident.

By far the worst case I ever handled involved a four-year-old boy I'll call Aiden. Beginning when Aiden was about three years old, his mother allowed men to pay her to sodomize her son. Eventually, Aiden was found walking alone in downtown Russellville, and that's when the local authorities and DHS got involved. Although he was four years old, Aiden could not speak; he just growled.

Aiden's mother was obviously mentally ill, and she eventually lost her parental rights. At least her son had a happy ending; Aiden was adopted by a loving couple. For some years afterward, the little boy sent me completed coloring book pages and I displayed them on the wall in my office.

Our local juvenile judges—elderly men, mostly—habitually appointed me to the worst abuse cases, like Aiden's. I now realize they were making an effort to run me out of town. Since I was the only 'lady lawyer' available, I was appointed to these cases. I therefore had to listen to how children were ignored, neglected, or physically and emotionally abused. Of course, I was paid very little for taking on these challenges.

Another case involved two little girls—sisters—in the early elementary grades. The girls had been born a couple of years apart. Their mother and father had separated; the mother had become so afraid of father that she finally abandoned both girls to his care, strange though that sounds. The girls' biological father then met another woman and married her. Both parents raped the two girls; the stepmother passed along her oral gonorrhea as well. Both father and stepmother went to prison for molesting the children. The two girls were young enough that they were adopted together into a good home and did well.

Another pair of sisters were so neglected by parents that both developed trench foot. The condition, which plagued many of our soldiers in the Vietnam War era, likely resulted from jamming damp feet into ill-fitting shoes. The parents, who were alcoholics, had simply failed to properly feed and clothe the little girls. Both kids were seriously underweight and malnourished. With some effort, I moved the children into a good foster home. Both sisters were eventually adopted.

At home in the evenings and on the weekends, I would gaze at my own son, watch Kane's infectious smile as he played, and realize how fortunate Bob and I were. Our boy was certainly loved and he was very well cared for.

For four years, I was the only local female attorney and the child abuse cases kept coming my way. I eventually stopped taking the cases because I could not bear to hear about the abuse or neglect of babies and preschoolers. The sort of disgust required to turn your back on such situations is a process and takes a while to develop, but I finally got there. Turning my back on innocent victims was not easy, but it was something I had to do.

Back then, my part of Arkansas was transforming itself. Heretofore, female lawyers would drive from Little Rock to Russellville and other county seats to appear before local judges. The judges did not react well to these female interlopers. At that point, many local judges were still hearing cases in which one of the attorneys was a relative, so time was needed to move our local judiciary into the modern world.

This sort of bold prejudice certainly extended to me. Out of sympathy for the deadbeat dads, the male Pope County Sheriff's deputies and local police officers simply refused to execute 'body attachments' to arrest fathers and enforce hard-won child support orders. When I walked into the law library while waiting for my case to be heard, the older male attorneys there would not acknowledge me. My contemporaries always spoke to me or said hello, but the older guys seemed to have a problem with a woman in their midst. Judges would treat me differently from other lawyers. I had to wait until the end of the docket to have my cases heard. At the time, I remember thinking that perhaps the judges were just trying to help me understand the court process as a sort of continuing legal education. I'd been in practice for some months when the truth dawned on me: Some simply did not want me in their court. From the start, I wasn't welcome.

I remember one occasion when, during a trial, our municipal judge told me I could not object again. I'd been appointed to defend a misdemeanor client, who deserved a fair trial like anyone else. The prosecutor was leading his own witness, which is not allowed. I objected, but the prosecutor kept leading. When I objected again, the judge told me to be quiet and stop objecting. I was clearly in the right, and I'd never felt that sort of outrage before. In many ways, that moment was the low point of my law career. The simple truth, however, was that the judge and many of his male colleagues knew no other way to deal with a woman in their court.

I am stubborn, however, and I know that 95 percent of all failure comes from quitting. So, I refused to quit. Other attorneys could view me in one of two ways, I decided: Either as a thorn in their side, or someone who was, like them, interested in helping clients. For a few years, I think most of the older male lawyers in Russellville saw me as the former. Then, as other women lawyers began to work in our part of Arkansas, my colleagues began to see me as a capable advocate.

But the glass ceiling still required a reckoning. Like most of our professional businessmen at the time, I wanted to join a civic club like Lions or Rotary. This, I thought, would allow me to volunteer in the community and make business contacts. At that time, however, you couldn't just join a club … you had to be invited. I sat about garnering an invitation. I first approached our Municipal Judge, Richard Peel, and asked if he would sponsor me as a Kiwanian. In 1994, there were no women in the Russellville Kiwanis Club. Richard told me that if he sponsored me, the other Kiwanians would likely kick him out of the chapter.

I then approached a friend who was in Lions Club. At that time, there were no women in the club. The only way a woman got into the Russellville Lions Club was by transferring from another club. If my friend sponsored me, he'd be blacklisted, or so he said.

I asked Rotarian Travis Adams, a colleague of my father's, to sponsor me as a Rotarian. He told me there were already too many attorneys in the Russellville Rotary Club. I told him they lacked a lady lawyer, but that made no difference.

I wound up waiting for the Kiwanis club to invite other women, and one of those women sponsored me into the Kiwanis club. I finally became a Kiwanian in May, 1998, and was secretary for the club for 25 years. I was Kiwanian of the Year in 2023.

One of my fellow Kiwanians, Linn Beebe, gave me what I call a 'courage plaque.' Linn told me that any woman who had the courage to break the 'glass ceiling' erected by my male colleagues deserved a medal of some sort. The back of the plaque says:

Dedicated to all those who have
the courage to face adversity
with a conquering spirit.

I still have the little plaque, and I look at it often, always remembering the chill I felt when Linn told me why I deserved to receive it.

Years ago, when I was just beginning my career, Judge Mobley told my colleagues that I wasn't a 'lady lawyer.' I was just an attorney. In society today, of course, 'lady lawyers' are no longer an oddity. The glass ceiling that once helped maintain the status quo in our the state is a thing of the past now; I helped shatter it. Women like me blazed a trail that others could follow, and I'm sure all of us are still quite proud of that.

CHAPTER THREE

The Divorce Queen

My mother raised me with the admonition that my family did not get divorced. That's why I decided to be a consumer and environmental law advocate rather than a divorce attorney. For that reason, I did not take any family law classes in law school. But because I was the only lady lawyer around when I hung up my shingle, people flocked to me to file their divorces.

I was also hired to fight for custody of their children, collect child support and resolve visitation problems. I effectively became the 'divorce queen' of Pope County. I was able to rationalize it all because I did not break up the blissful union. The marriage was usually irrevocably broken by the time the client came to my office.

Surprisingly, I had as many men as women hire me to file their divorce or handle their custody dispute. Sometimes, the husband and wife would fight over who would be represented by me! The man would often call for free legal advice as a way to tie me up; if I had a conflict of interest, which would be the case if I offered the husband legal guidance, then I could not represent the wife.

I quickly surmounted that problem by declining to offer free legal advice.

Many of these folks came into my office looking visibly apprehensive. For some reason, people viewed the experience of consulting with me as something akin to going to the dentist. Having a fear of dentists myself, I never understood what was so scary about coming to chat with an attorney. I gave no shots, and I had no drills. I do admit to having to 'drill' for truth now and then, which I suppose can be a painful process for some people.

One of those visibly apprehensive folks was a woman who was sharing her bed with a gentle whitetail deer. When Rita came to my office and told me that she slept with a doe, I immediately surmised that her marriage was on the rocks. Three is a crowd, particularly if they aren't all the same species. Rita was a tall blonde; she told me that she had not slept with her husband in quite some time. She preferred her pet doe as a bed companion.

"Does the doe live with you?" I asked. The arrangement sounded unusual to me and I admit I was a bit puzzled.

"Yes," Rita replied quietly, "she is perfectly housebroken. When she needs to go outside, she just goes out the screen door." Apparently, the deer did better than some of my 'housebroken' dogs.

During my first years in practice, I would often ask about the issue or problems in the marriage. After I'd been in practice for 20 years or so, I didn't ask, and hopefully, prospective clients didn't tell! The woman with the doe in her bed made for interesting conversation with my husband. Neither Bob nor I could figure out where the hooves would go.

Since there was little property in dispute, I got that divorce done in record time—just 32 days from the day I filed the Complaint for Divorce with the court. In Arkansas, a divorce can be accomplished in 30 days, but you have to serve the opposing party before that 30 day clock can start running. In this case, we served the woman's husband two days after we filed.

I'm unsure how the relationship with the housebroken doe wound down, but I do know that Rita was happily divorced. She was a quiet woman with soft brown eyes. I'd say she had doe eyes, but I try to avoid cheap laughs.

Then there was Tricia, who came into my office visibly excited. I had represented her on other matters; she'd come in to tell me that she had met a wonderful man on a well-known dating website. My first thought: He might be a woman who had a sex change and became a man. Tricia would know no different. She and this gentleman had been emailing each other for two months. This was in an era when internet and email were widely available but cellphones were not; at that time, long distance telephone calls were still expensive.

Tricia, a rather plump, bubbly redhead, was happy that she'd met her soulmate. Needless to say, I wasn't quite as certain ... especially since Tricia had not yet spoken to the guy on the phone. Could Tricia really be in love with someone she'd only met online? Amazingly, this was happening more often than I realized.

A couple of months later, Tricia was back in my office. She told me that Rick, her beloved, was due to arrive in Russellville the following week. The kicker: Tricia and Rick were planning to be married the day after Rick got to town. I tried to talk some sense to Tricia, and asked if she really knew Rick at all. He could be using a fake name, or he might be a serial killer. Her mother and sister were all telling her the same thing, she said; we might as well have been speaking to a brick wall. Tricia wasn't listening to anyone.

Rick arrived from Arizona, and he and Tricia were married by a Justice of the Peace the following morning. Since Tricia had been a long-time client, she came back through my door again about two months later. The sad news: Rick was a Persian Gulf vet, had PTSD and was very abusive. Tricia asked me to get her a 'quickie' divorce. Since she and Rick had been married only a short time, I might have gotten her an annulment with fraud as the grounds. However, Tricia opted for a simple divorce. Needless to say, I wasn't at all surprised. Fortunately, this was an easy divorce; there was no property to divide.

My record time for finalizing a divorce decree and getting my client divorced was 31 days. We would file the divorce complaint the day the client came into the office and serve the defendant in person by the following day. That's what I came to think of as a quick divorce! Of course, all divorces did not wind up sad and depressing. I had about 30 clients get divorced and then reconcile within a few weeks or a few months. My embarrassed client would tell me that they and their spouse were "talking," which typically meant that they were sleeping together again. I would dismiss the case as soon as the client came in to sign the Order of Dismissal.

I had my clients come to the office to sign the order in person. Once, the husband's girlfriend—the husband was the defendant in this particular case—called my office and told me that my client and the defendant had reconciled. She called pretending to be my client's wife, when, in fact, she was the defendant's girlfriend. The defendant was attempting to have the case dismissed, and the trick did not work.

Sometimes, couples required two or three years to come by and sign the order. I learned to be quite patient. When I retired in 2020, I had a number of old, inactive files sitting in my file cabinets. At any one time, I estimate that I had over 300 active cases. Herding cats would have been far easier than managing my client list at any given time.

Interestingly, some clients who filed for divorce remarried their former husband or wife and the process would repeat itself. Unlike other attorneys, I did not stir up cases to make more money. As a result, a number of my clients actually reconciled. The most interesting case of this nature involved a husband who got divorced, and the marital property was divided up. Then the parties reconciled, and the couple lived together happily for the rest of their lives.

I was always thrilled to see clients reconcile. These reunited couples gave me hope, believe it or not. In a way, the reconciliations kept me handling divorces, always looking forward to a more positive outcome.

There were, however, some cases in which reconciliation wasn't a viable option. Marla's situation is one of those that comes to mind; the marriage was simply too far gone to save, and none of that was Marla's fault.

As soon as Marla walked into my office and sat down, I could tell that she was blind in one eye. She told me that her husband, a local surgeon, had caused an automobile accident and that she'd lost her eye in the wreck. She now had a glass eye, but it looked pretty convincing.

As it happened, Marla's husband's nurse was pregnant—the surgeon was the father—and Marla had him dead to rights. Marla's husband, Jack, hadn't filed for a divorce. In an effort to work things out, Marla had thought to try counseling. Dr. Jack, however, was adamant that he was in love with his nurse. When he and Marla had married, the husband had a boy and a younger girl. Marla had stayed at home with the children; she'd been like their mother. The real mother never contacted them. Now that Jack had committed adultery, Marla could see why! The mother wanted nothing to do with her former husband.

Jack was already divorced when he and Marla met. Following the somewhat customary seven-year cycle, the surgeon had traded in his old wife for a new model. As it happened, the judge in the case was an old-fashioned type who had been married quite a few years. When the judge heard that Jack had gotten his nurse pregnant—in a small town, rumors fly around like plastic grocery bags blown by a gale—and things didn't go well for the good doctor.

In that particular case, I received over $20,000 in court-ordered legal fees that Jack had to pay directly to me. Since he was making a good income, Marla received a nice alimony check each month. Once again, the divorce queen of Pope County had triumphed on the side of the right.

I had noticed that when I filed a divorce action or a petition for legal separation on behalf of a female client, her husband did not want to have a duel with me. However, when a male attorney filed a divorce for a woman, the husband felt that the attorney was keeping his wife from him … and perhaps sleeping with her! I was very lucky, because I had some nasty divorces wherein the husband really did not want me to get his wife a divorce. I survived them all unscathed.

When I began my law practice, divorce court in Russellville was held every Thursday morning. The attorneys all met in the library at the courthouse before court began. We gossiped and drank coffee. Years ago, divorce court was often referred to by local lawyers as "Mother's Day." Chancery Judge Richard Mobley almost always awarded custody to the mother, regardless of the circumstances. No matter what the husband and wife earned, he typically awarded attorney's fees and costs to the wife, so the husband almost always had to pay fees of about $300 and costs of $50 or so.

Sometimes, going to weekly divorce court was more entertaining than watching a soap opera on television. While divorce clients had to wait outside the courtroom and were called in to testify, attorneys could remain seated in the courtroom jury box throughout the proceedings. One day, another local attorney—I'll call him Steve—put a wife on the stand, and the woman had to testify and prove grounds for divorce. While some states allow no-fault divorce, in Arkansas, the party seeking the divorce had to prove he or she had grounds, such as general indignities.

Steve was going through the usual boring questions with his client. He asked her to state her name, address, date of marriage and date of separation. He asked her about the couple's children. When a spouse filed for divorce in the 1980s, Arkansas law required them to live separate and apart during the proceedings, or the case would be dismissed. After the case was adjudicated, the parties could cohabitate and have sexual relations, but they had to separate to get the case settled first.

Steve then asked his next question: "Have you had sex with a man since you filed for this divorce?" His sweet client looked at him and said, "Only with you, Steve." The lawyers sitting in the jury box could not help but smirk. Of course, Judge Mobley granted the nice lady's divorce.

I do remember the most difficult divorce I ever encountered. Sarah had been married to Bruce since Sarah was 15 years old. Bruce was 25 years older, and Sarah's mother had finally consented to allow her daughter to wed. At that time, Sarah thought that being married to Bruce was better than being stuck at home.

Bruce, a survivalist and White supremacist, lived with Sarah in the hills north of the small town of Dover, Arkansas. He had an arsenal of guns, other weapons like grenades, and a stock of supplies laid in to survive the forthcoming apocalypse.

I'd never actually been scared of the party on the other side of a divorce case, but Bruce was different. His cold stare chilled me. I very nearly told Sarah I could not take her case. However, Sarah had a daughter who needed to be protected from Bruce, who was apparently an abusive dad. In the end, my concern for the child won out. I typically took divorce and custody cases mostly to protect and serve the children who were stuck in the middle.

I got Sarah divorced, and she received custody of the daughter. Bruce, meanwhile, got another teenager pregnant. Because he now had another child to support, Bruce stopped making child support payments to Sarah. He stopped performing any work for which we could discover an income. I assumed Bruce was doing work 'under the table' for cash.

Sarah had to take Bruce back to court to collect the child support he owed and to terminate Bruce's visitation rights. The judge put Bruce in jail for failure to pay child support and terminated his access to Sarah's daughter.

While I never had an actual problem with Bruce, I did have a problem communicating with his attorney. His lawyer would never answer my interrogatories—very pointed, personal questions about where he worked, how much he made, what his monthly bills were, and so forth—and the judge finally entered an order finding Bruce in contempt and awarding me attorney's fees.

Despite the father's wayward nature, Sarah's daughter grew into a fine young woman.

Sometimes, from the outset of a divorce case, I found myself baffled by the way a woman picked the father for her child. Lucy was a plump, fluffy-haired, blue-eyed doll. She was also pregnant when she met Michael and they fell in love. The sweet baby boy, born after their marriage, was named after Michael. However, the blissful union failed when the boy turned three. The boy knew his name and the man he thought was his daddy.

When Lucy came to my office to file a divorce, she explained that Michael was not the biological father of her son. Both mother and father knew this to be the case. She decided to have a DNA test to prove Michael could not be the father; as expected, the test proved this point. Lucy didn't know who the actual father might be; she had slept with three men in a single month and no longer remembered anyone's name. These were one-night stands; she'd met the men in bars.

Michael was quite upset. He would no longer be the father figure his little boy loved. His attorney fought hard to keep Michael close to his son. But by law, the boy wasn't Michael's. If a child is born during a marriage, the mother places her husband's name on the birth certificate as the father of the child.

When I began practicing law, there was Lord Mansfield's Rule, which was an 18th-Century law followed by most American jurisdictions until some years ago. Lord Mansfield's Rule stated that if a child was born during a marriage, the child was presumed to be the legitimate issue of the marriage. Even in a divorce, no one could delegitimize the child. This was in the best interest of the child, of course. One older judge would tell me, "Lord Mansfield would turn over in his grave today" whenever we delegitimatized a child during a divorce proceeding.

In Lucy's case, the law was clear: The boy was not Michael's son. Michael had no rights as a father. Then again, he didn't have to pay child support when Lucy won custody of the little boy.

Kelsey came to see me about a real marital dilemma. Her husband of a decade had just received a 20-year sentence for burglary and theft. The young man had already begun serving his time in the Tucker Maximum Security unit near Pine Bluff, Arkansas. The couple had two children—Max, who was 7, and 5-year-old Lacey.

Kelsey had decided she didn't want to be married to her incarcerated husband. Getting a client divorced from a spouse in the slam wasn't particularly difficult; I'd even handled cases where the wife was in prison and the husband was at home with the kids.

I told Kelsey to avoid any contact with her husband, and urged her to refrain from taking the children to see their father in prison. All I needed to do was send the appropriate paperwork to the warden at Tucker Max. The warden would serve Kelsey's husband with the summons and complaint. I would receive proof that the inmate had been legally served.

Kelsey breathed a sigh of relief when the papers had been served. The husband didn't answer the complaint, and in about 60 days, the couple were divorced. Kelsey was given custody of the children. I told her it might be better to avoid having the children visit their father, and she followed my advice until the children got older.

Once or twice, the inmate answered the divorce complaint, and the sheriff's office had to transport him more than 100 miles to the divorce hearing. Usually, the inmate walked away from the divorce with his personal property and not much else. Sometimes, he was awarded prison visitation, but that usually depended on circumstances and the age and maturity of the children involved.

I'll never forget the day Suzy walked into my office. The woman looked so … well, defeated. She was attractive enough, with auburn hair and soft green eyes, but there was an element of despair in her manner. Suzy told me she needed to file for divorce. I asked the usual questions—name, name of the husband, names and ages of the children—before asking why she wanted the divorce.

Suzy and her husband had lived together for nearly 8 years before they were married. At that point, they'd been married just over 2 years. The couple had 3 children together … a girl, 6, and twin boys, age 3. Suzy said cohabitation was a walk in the park, but after marriage, her husband had changed.

Doug, she said, used to drink a couple of beers as he watched football on Sunday afternoons. Now, she told me, he drank a case of beer over the weekend. Because he was inebriated over the weekend, he didn't share care of their children. In fact, Doug was given to going out 'fishing with the boys' on Saturday mornings and didn't return until Sunday night. He drank so much that he once wet their bed.

In Arkansas, habitual drunkenness is a ground for divorce. Suzy certainly had no problem proving grounds! I was astounded that Suzy hadn't discovered her basic incompatibility with Doug during the 8 years they were living together. I suppose her case goes to show that living together before marriage doesn't always guarantee you'll live happily ever after.

Lilly, a sweet woman with brown hair and clear green eyes, came into my office one sunny Spring afternoon. She wanted to know about her rights under the law if she should file for divorce. Lilly had been married for 6 years, she told me, and she'd reached the end of her rope.

I gathered the usual information and then tried to get to the bottom of the issue. Lilly's husband, a minister, ran a home for men with substance abuse issues. While he and Lilly were dating, the husband displayed great self-control. He'd kiss and cuddle, but told Lilly that fornication was a sin.

Hours following the blessed event, the couple were ready for bed. Lilly was surprised that her husband had showered and donned full battle armor—heavy pajamas—and was soon snoring in bed. In the days that followed, Lilly discovered that her marriage would never be consummated—there would be no sex. The blushing bride got a hug and a peck on the cheek when her husband left for work in the mornings, but nothing else was forthcoming.

Fast-forward 6 years, and Lilly sat in my office crying. I found her to be much more understanding and accepting than I would have been, had I been the client. Her simple divorce was quickly over, and Lilly got on with her life. I'm still amazed that she remained faithful within a sexless marriage for so many years.

As I write this chapter, 3 states allow no-fault divorces. In other words, couples can obtain a divorce without having to show fault on one side or the other. When I retired in early 2020, Arkansas still required the plaintiff in a divorce action to prove grounds for divorce.

'Grounds' is a loose term. The easiest 'grounds' to prove are what Arkansas law refers to as 'general indignities,' when your spouse makes your life so intolerable that you can no longer remained married. Other grounds were pretty specific: Adultery, alcohol abuse or abandonment for 18 months or longer.

Gloria came into my office rather distraught. She and Steve had 5 children together; the eldest was 8 years old. Gloria was a nurse practitioner and Steve was a dentist. During his work week, Dr. Steve had many attractive women in his chair. He also had an addiction to sex, alcohol and gambling.

If the woman turned him on, Steve found that he couldn't resist. And each time, Gloria found out. When Steve faithfully promised not to even *look* at another woman again, his fidelity was short-lived. Within a few months, he would be back in another adulterous relationship.

The financial devastation was even worse. Steve would take the money he and Gloria had earned and hit the blackjack tables at Tunica, Mississippi. Along the way, he consumed copious amounts of beer. After patient online searching, Gloria found a special center where they treated individuals like Steve who were dealing with multiple addictions. Steve was admitted and began his stint in rehab.

Unfortunately, Steve chose to leave the rehab center before his treatment plan had gathered much steam. Steve apparently felt he had to return to his practice. He hadn't been back long before he started yet another affair.

Gloria had had enough. One child was still a minor, but 4 were above the age of 18. I filed the divorce, and Gloria was awarded custody of the minor daughter. The couple split their real and personal property without much wrangling. Gloria became a good friend, and I hoped she would find a kind, faithful man. That sort of guy seems rare in today's society.

In 2018, Arkansas legalized same-sex marriage. I knew that the divorce rate would soar; the new law was a goldmine for attorneys like me. I said as much when the law was enacted.

Ginny was sexually frustrated and generally unhappy. She and Sophia were fighting over their pair of Yorkshire Terriers, among other things. After child custody issues, I found that animals caused the most fights during divorce proceedings.

Unlike Ginny, Sophia did not bother to hire an attorney. The first hearing, a temporary hearing, temporarily sets custody, visitation, spousal support, if any, and more importantly, the temporary division of real and personal property. Real property, of course, is land; personal property encompasses about everything else.

The law also provides for 'mixed property,' but I have never been able to determine what 'mixed' property really is. Nor could my law school instructors. A mobile home with a deck attached might be construed as mixed property, since the home can still be moved. Another example might be the data stored on a computer used by both spouses. If you can successfully divide either of those, you are doing better than me.

Anyway, Sophia was upset that Ginny had dared to file a divorce proceeding against her and went on the warpath, calling my secretary and wanting to speak with me. Of course, my secretary took the brunt of Sophia's anger. I notified the Circuit Judge's assistant that I would need the bailiff to keep these two ladies separated on divorce court day. Otherwise, a catfight would likely ensue.

The other attorneys appeared for court and wondered what all the hubbub was about. Sophia had to be escorted into the courtroom by the bailiff. I stuck by Ginny like glue, even accompanying her to the restroom.

The hearing went well enough, and the Yorkies were temporarily placed with Sophia. That one factor calmed the combatants considerably. The two women were finally divorced a year later after a hotly contested final hearing.

Dogs were easy enough to handle, but another divorce involved a ferret. Kayla was a cute brunette without much in the way of common sense. She and her husband had absolutely no property to fight over. They decided to have a contested divorce over a ferret and a pair of Donny Osmond tickets. By the time they were divorced, the Donny Osmond concert had already come and gone, so neither party got to go. Kayla's husband, Steve, wound up with the ferret, which had been a gift to the young couple.

These odd custody battles were a piece of cake in comparison to the battles parents fought to retain control of their children.

When people called out of the blue and asked questions about divorce or custody issues, they would most often ask the age at which the child got to choose with which parent the child would live. My short answer: There is no age. Even if the child is 17, the judge's decision is always made on the basis of the best interest of the child. Judges do not even let teenagers decide where they want to live, or with whom. This is probably as it should be. Parents are not above bribing their children with promises of new cars or sound systems, for example.

Steve was a large, dark-haired man with green eyes. He was a father of two boys and seemed normal enough when he walked into my office. He completed my standard questionnaire listing his name, address, occupation and so forth. When Steve mentioned that he had two sons, I told him I needed their dates of birth and Social Security numbers. The first son was Xavier, which was a common enough name at the time. Steve said that the second son was named Zander Zombie.

I thought perhaps my hearing was faulty, and asked Steve to repeat his son's name. Why, I wondered, would anyone want to name a sweet, innocent baby Zombie? Of course, I didn't want to offend Steve, so I stayed silent for a few moments.

As it happened, the divorce went off without significant issue. Steve and his wife shared custody of the two boys, with the mother having primary or physical custody. The parents wanted joint custody with each parent keeping the boys half the time. Of course, the parent who had primary custody actually wound up making the majority of decisions about the children.

CHAPTER FOUR

On Custody

Typically, non-custodial parents had their children every other weekend and on half of the major holidays. Non-custodial parents were usually allotted six weeks during the summer as well, which worked until all-year schools began popping up. At that time, men were seldom awarded full custody. In a typical joint custody case, the other parent would have a tough time moving off to New York or California. If a client came in after their divorce and wanted to move out of state with the children born during the marriage, we'd file a petition and serve the other party.

I remember one true joint custody case in which my client, Johnny, had a particularly difficult time. His ex-wife had filed a petition to move the two children out of the state. The girl was 12 years old, and the boy was 10. Johnny did not want his children to be relocated to Tulsa, Oklahoma, almost 200 miles removed from Pope County. At that point, he had both children every day after school and from Friday night to Sunday night every other weekend.

Johnny and his wife had agreed to the strict joint custody schedule during the divorce process. In the two-day custody hearing, the mother opposed my client by telling the court that he had not been a diligent father. When school started each fall, the mother took the two kids to open house. She kept track of their school homework. The dad did attend some of the parent-teacher conferences, but these were typically separate conferences because the former husband and wife had never gotten along.

Johnny's ex-wife then remarried. Her new husband could only work in a big city. At that time, Russellville's population was more than 28,000. The new husband had a good-paying job in Tulsa, and Johnny's ex could make more money there as well.

The children, however, had lived in Pope County, Arkansas their entire lives. Their grandparents—Johnny's parents—were nearby, and often took the children to the dentist or other appointments. The grandparents essentially helped raise the kids.

The 10-year-old boy had a lazy eye, was a candidate for surgery, and could look forward to growing up cured of the ailment. The boy was self-conscious about his appearance; he wanted to have the surgery.

Since the father and mother shared custody, they needed to agree if—and where—the boy would have the surgery. Johnny was supposed to accompany his son to an office visit with a practitioner in Little Rock, but he missed the appointment due to work. Johnny had to make a delivery and could not make the 75-mile trip in time. Consequently, he did not get his son's medical records, nor did he actually speak with the physician.

Plainly, Johnny was leery of his boy having the surgery because the cosmetic outcome was less than certain. The judge, however, ruled that Johnny had kept his son from having a necessary surgery and had missed the children's school open house that fall and for the five years preceding.

The mother had clearly handled much of the actual caregiving while Johnny was at work providing for himself and his kids. Consequently, the judge ruled that the best interests of the children would be served by granting the mother full custody, enabling her to move herself and the kids to Oklahoma.

Johnny was crestfallen. He decided to appeal the judge's ruling and set up a website to raise money for the appeal. I told Johnny he had little chance of success. If there are valid reasons for the ruling, judges are given wide discretion in custody cases. Chancery judges rule in the best interests of the children, and in these cases, the law is a fluid thing.

Together with his live-in girlfriend, Johnny sold t-shirts and solicited donations aimed at keeping his children in Arkansas. The opposing attorney filed a motion to shut down the website, since the site contained a good deal of negative information about the children's mother. The judge signed the order and the fundraising website was shut down. The children moved to Oklahoma with their mother and stepfather.

One fascinating custody case involved a lovely Black woman, tall and willowy. I'll call her Louise. Louise was built to have babies! When Joe came to hire me, Louise had already borne six children. Joe was White and had an adorable little boy with chocolate brown eyes and a melt-your-heart smile. Isaac was five; he was ready to start kindergarten.

Joe and Louise were never married, but DNA testing proved Joe was the father. I say the test 'proved' paternity because the test results were slightly qualified: There was a 99.9999% probability that Joe was the father.

Louise had several problems. On her bucket list, Louise had written a goal to have babies with men of all races. Except having a baby with an Asian man, Louise had accomplished that objective. Incidentally, Louise was very pregnant during our hearing.

When Joe went to get his boy for visitation, the boy's shoes could not be found. The house was in disarray; it looked as if it had been struck by a tornado. There were too few rooms in Louise's home for her six children, herself and another adult. Her children were somewhat neglected.

I filed for change of custody, which resulted in a two-day courtroom custody fight. Louise and her attorney fought hard, but the facts were stacked against them. The judge awarded Joe sole custody of his son. Louise was given restricted visitation due to her busy schedule and lack of attention. The other five children remained in the home.

There's good news and bad news about a custody fight: The good news is that the children have parents who obviously love their kids very much. Both parents want the children to live with them, to the exclusion of the other parent.

The bad news is twofold: There's no legal age at which a child can pick which parent. Coincidentally, there's also no minimum age at which a child can be called as a witness.

To win a custody fight, a parent will sometimes call their young child as a witness. I've seen children as young as six years old put on the stand to testify. The problem is that the child's answers are unpredictable, especially in a closed hearing. A child can only be 'coached' to a point. The parents are asked to step outside the courtroom while the child is being questioned.

The judge always talks with the child, asks about their general and scholastic welfare, and tells them to pay no attention to the lawyers sitting across the way. The judge does his or her best to determine whether the child is old enough to understand the difference between telling the truth and telling a lie. The child usually sits on the witness stand while being questioned. Without the parents present, the child can become an interesting conversationalist. Either attorney can relay to the parent what the child said, of course, or the parents can purchase a transcript of the testimony.

Even if the mom and dad are getting along, a custody dispute starts a war. The children are caught in the middle. The fight inevitably turns nasty, rendering the return to a normal family life impossible. Custody fights often reminded me of a broken bird's wing; things can never be put back as they were.

I remember a sad custody fight. The case began with a phone call from Cindy, who wanted to hire me even though she lived in Florida. Cindy was a tall, slim, attractive woman with dark, curly hair. She had custody of her two girls. Her ex-husband, Joe, who lived near Russellville, got the judge to sign an emergency order and got an *ex parte* order giving him temporary custody of their two girls. A Sheriff's Deputy went to Florida to execute the custody order; Joe accompanied him. Cindy and Joe had been divorced two years before.

Joe had remarried and his new wife was both intelligent and nurturing. Of course, Cindy wanted the girls returned to her as soon as possible. I filed an immediate answer objecting to the emergency change of custody. The case was very complicated, due to the fact that the younger girl had a condition marked by early onset of puberty. The little girl needed frequent hormone injections. At the age of five, she already had pubic hair and all the external indications of a pubescent girl.

Cindy had decided that the hormone treatments were either not working or too toxic for her daughter to tolerate. The little girl was seven years old. Joe took exception to Cindy's decision and asserted that stopping the treatment so suddenly was tantamount to neglect. Cindy did not wean the child from the treatment or consult a doctor before stopping it altogether. We went to divorce court and pleaded her case. The judge ruled that Joe would have temporary custody until all issues could be heard.

The custody fight that ensued was long and nasty. In the interim, the girls adjusted to living with their father and step-mother. The final hearing, held nearly a year later, required two entire calendar days. The judge ruled that Joe would have custody of the two minor children. Cindy had to pay child support, but she received visitation rights. Cindy was devastated; I'll never forget her sitting in my office saying, "I would rather have my girls dead than have them in their father's custody."

I was shocked, to say the least. I had lost my own 17-year-old son a few months earlier, and the pain of losing a child is extraordinarily severe. I told Cindy that she was blessed to still have her two children and to be able share some part of their lives. I could no longer share my son's life; he was gone with a permanence that defied my comprehension.

Child support cases are always sticky. The court typically orders the mother or father to pay child support. If the dad is awarded custody of two minor children, the mom has to pay child support for two minor dependents. The child support is based on the mom's take-home pay, inclusive of bonuses. The only way to escape paying significant child support is to work for cash under the table. Of course, no taxes are paid on under-the-table income.

I had a case in which the dad, a plumber, was ordered to pay child support for his three children. His tax return, filed jointly with the wife, showed that he netted about $20,000 for the year. Everyone involved in the case knew that this man made over $60,000 annually, because he supported a family of five. His income allowed his wife to stay home and take care of the house and three children. We could not prove what sort of income the husband *really* made, and he would not admit that he had cheated on his income taxes. The wife was effectively stuck with the $20,000 figure because she had signed their joint tax return, filed before they sought a divorce. She couldn't protest her husband's higher income without incriminating herself. We didn't squeeze much blood out of that turnip!

Child support orders are supposed to be strictly enforced. If a parent does not keep his child support current, he or she can go to jail for being in contempt. I saw cases where the husband owed more than $20,000 in back child support. In this particular case, the man was picked up on a 'body attachment' and put in jail until he paid a large amount of the arrearage.

England had debtor's prisons; in the United States, we abolished prison sentences for poverty. Being in prison for child support avoidance is probably the closest thing our country can manage. Every month or so, the deputy would bring the man back to court to see if the man's family could bond him out of jail. Sometimes, the family could be relied upon to pay some of the man's back child support. Since he could not work, the man would sit in jail for six to eight months.

In some states, like Indiana, failure to pay child support is a criminal felony. In other states, enforcing child support is still a haphazard process. Interestingly, if the man does not get to enjoy his established court-ordered visitation with the child, that is no excuse for failing to pay child support.

My clients could not understand this anomaly. The custodial parent—usually the mom—could be held in contempt, but was rarely jailed for failing to facilitate the visitation. I did see women jailed for failure to pay; the judge would tell them to bring their pajamas and toothbrush!

"Is there alimony in Arkansas?" That's what a stranger on the phone would ask me. They expected to get free legal advice over the phone. I always said, "Free advice is worth what you pay for it … nothing!" However, my response would be, "That all depends on the circumstances of the case. You'd need to make an appointment. I do have a minimum charge for a telephone or on-site consultation."

Quite often, the person on the other end hung up.

The interesting thing is that alimony became spousal support in the 1990s because women had to start paying alimony to men. Spousal support was supposed to be a gender-neutral phrase.

There are many factors for qualifying for alimony or spousal support. The first factor was if the man made more money than his wife, or vice-versa. Second was the length of the marriage. Third, whether there were children borne of the marriage. Fourth, how much child support is the person receiving in addition to alimony? Fifth, the amount of education the person has, especially if the person gave up going to college themselves so they could help put the spouse through college, law school or medical school.

Incidentally, I saw stay-at-home dads letting their wives work as attorneys or engineers and giving up their own careers to be a caregiver for their minor children. The professional would work long hours and leave the childrearing to the other spouse.

The sixth factor in determining alimony or child support revolved around the question of whether one of the parties had an affair during the marriage. After separating, a lot of the parties would move in with a new man or woman and get engaged to be married as soon as the ink was dry on the Decree of Divorce. Sometimes, they got married *before* the ink dried, when the divorce was not final. The newly-divorced person would find themselves married to two men or women, since the marriage occurred before the decree was file-marked in the clerk's office. When you are married to two people at the same time, it's called bigamy, and bigamy is a felony. I saw many a man or woman married to two people at once. I would quickly annul the second marriage. This was sad when a child had been born in the second marriage that had to be annulled.

An annulment cost as much as a divorce ... about $1000 in 2013. My clients always argued with me, and couldn't believe it cost as much to get a marriage annulled as it did to get divorced. However, they learned to let the ink dry on their divorce decree before they thought about getting married again!

I always warned newly-divorced clients to wait 30 days after the divorce decree was file-marked before getting married again. Some, of course, chose to plunge in and got married anyway.

Black's Law Dictionary defines bigamy as "the criminal offense of willfully and knowingly contracting a second marriage while the first marriage, to the knowledge of the offender, is still subsisting and undissolved." Examples of bigamy include a man with two wives, or a woman with two husbands living.

In canon law, on the other hand, bigamy denotes the offense committed by an ecclesiastical priest who was married to two wives successively. Polygamy might be committed by marrying a second wife after the death of the first, or by marrying a widow.

My client, Marylou, was quite surprised to discover that her husband was already married to another woman. His excuse: His attorney had told John that his decree of divorce was entered with the court, and that John could get remarried. John and Marylou ran to the courthouse to get a marriage license. Happily married, they then decided to have a baby.

The couple named their new daughter Mary. While the new parents were still adjusting to all the changes in their world, John's first wife called Marylou and told her that the divorce decree from John's first marriage had never been entered. Marylou was in a bad spot. She didn't want a divorce on religious grounds. I certainly understood that, but I explained that the real problem lay in the new baby. If I annulled the marriage, which was actually void under the law, then John and Marylou's child would have been born out of wedlock.

I managed this little hat trick by getting John's first marriage dissolved, then I got an annulment for John and Marylou. They were remarried in another ceremony. I asked the prosecuting attorney if he intended to file charges against John. He replied in the negative. Then he added, "Mistakes do happen."

When someone asks me to tell them about the worst clients I had, Shirley springs to mind. She was angry about phonograph records and an ancient Victrola. When she took the stand, the judge seemed to take an almost immediate dislike. I asked for a brief recess and got it, intent on hustling Shirley out of the courthouse to try to determine why the judge was so ... well, *disinterested.*

The court reporter grabbed at my jacket as I was heading out. "Your client has extreme body odor," she told me. Because I have absolutely no sense of smell, that little sidebar conversation stunned me. In point of fact, it explained a lot: When I would meet with clients who had poor hygiene, smelled strongly of sweat or stale cigarette smoke, I never noticed anything. I always wondered why my secretaries rushed into my office with cans of Lysol. They'd spray down my office first, then the reception room.

That day, I walked back into the courtroom with my eyes wide open. Since the part of my brain that detects odors doesn't work, my nasal passages are inoperative. In this particular case, I was glad for that! *Let this be a lesson to you,* I thought to myself. *Some clients just stink.*

I retired from my law practice because Arkansas passed the Open Carry firearms law. I was having a peaceful day in my office when a tall, brawny man came in for a scheduled appointment. When I greeted him, I noticed something of immediate interest: A handgun strapped to his thigh. He had a two-year-old son and another child on the way. Many divorces commenced during a pregnancy.

Perhaps the husband didn't want the second or third child. In this particular case, the husband noted that his wife had gained about 50 pounds during the pregnancy. This seemed to be the root cause of his problem. I mentioned several times the inadvisability of having a handgun near small children.

A couple of weeks later, the man told me he'd sold the handgun and bought a Labrador Retriever. I honestly felt that I'd been called to serve in a way that might have saved the lives of two children.

By the time I'd been in practice for a decade or so, other lady lawyers were hanging up their shingle. I was glad to have the company, but quite often, differences between myself and the newer female attorneys were rather stark. For example, one woman's father had a successful practice; she made the fourth attorney in her father's firm. In contrast, I had started with very little money and no real practical experience.

As it happened, handling divorce and custody cases was a challenge, and it provided me with all the practical experience I ever wanted ... and then some. I was often called the 'divorce queen' of my part of the State, and I'd earned that distinction the hard way.

CHAPTER FIVE

Sweet Inspiration

Coco Chanel said, "Dress shabbily and they remember the dress; dress impeccably and they remember the woman."

Coco's sage advice was compounded when, at the outset of my law career, I read *Dress for Success* by John T. Molloy. I must have needed help with my wardrobe and appearance, for my mother bought me Molloy's book and forcefully suggested I read it.

So, how *does* a lady lawyer dress for success? Molloy's guidance was straightforward and to the point: In the South, professional women might wear grey, navy or black pinstriped suits with a skirt. Further into his book, Molloy opined that women in my part of the country might also wear an emerald green suit. Since I have hazel eyes, emerald green suits made my eyes look *quite* green. I had three very nice green suits.

Beneath the suit, the shirt or blouse might be pink, blue or white. To top off the ensemble, I bought scarves that tied in a bow, rather like a man's bow tie. Typically, the scarves were yellow, burgundy and blue.

I wore glasses, which I thought made me look more intelligent. I tried contacts, but I was constantly putting eye drops in my eyes. Finally, an ophthalmologist tested my eyes, which was a rather painful experience. Through my tears, I told the man that I obviously did *not* have dry eyes. My remonstrations made no real difference; I still could not wear contacts. With the glasses, the overall effect was slightly more professorial than I'd have liked, but I carried it off rather well. I walked into the courtroom looking for all the world like a female version of Perry Mason.

I remember receiving a memo from Judge Richard Gardner which instructed all attorneys to appear in court wearing a coat and tie. Some of my male counterparts had apparently been dressing in a rather casual manner ... too casual for the judge, anyway. Many neglected to wear a jacket, a tie, or both!

I thought Judge Gardner's memo was too funny for words. At the time, I seriously considered wearing a man's sport jacket and tie to court, but I never got up the nerve. I would be reminded of Judge Gardner's memo in years to come when I had to ask male clients to remove their hats or ball caps once inside the courtroom. A courtroom is akin to a sanctuary, but some old habits die hard.

Even on days when I wasn't in court, I wore a suit, skirt and jacket. I only wore pants in wintertime when it was very cold or when snow threatened. Only after a decade in practice did I begin wearing pantsuits. I bought a bright pink suit with a skirt and a purple wrap-around dress; both were bright and cheery.

Typically, our divorce judges would have court on Halloween. To get into the spirit of the occasion, I dressed in my hot pink and black-striped tights with a short black skirt and pink blouse. I would get wolf whistles as I walked around downtown. The judges would always laugh at what they called my "law suit."

When other lady lawyers appeared on the scene in the 1990s, they were often wearing a cocktail dress and spike heels. I was already fairly tall, over 5' 7", and didn't need more than a one-inch heel. In law school, my classmates had often been men who were 5' 6" to 5' 8". I'm not a psychologist, but I honestly thought these young men wanted the power, prestige and other rewards of a law practice to make up for their relatively short stature.

Nine months of pregnancy have a unique way of creating challenges for a lady lawyer committed to looking like a professional. In

1989, I bought navy jumpers and a black maternity dress ... all so I could look like a lawyer. I wore bright, perky scarves to liven up the dark clothing. When I was five months' pregnant and showing, my colleague Bunny Bullock asked me if I were pregnant. I proudly replied in the affirmative. "Well, you're always so thin," Bunny replied, "and I wondered why you were gaining weight!"

I gained 38 pounds while I was pregnant, and after Kane was born, I nursed him for a year. I eventually lost the extra weight, and I went back to work six weeks after my son's arrival. Juggling a family and a law practice was hard work, and I survived on very little sleep for the first three years. While I never regretted having a husband and child, I did wonder from time to time whether I'd live through the experience!

Coco Chanel and John T. Molloy helped me look the part of a lady lawyer, but Perry Mason had inspired me to *be* an attorney. My boyfriend often says he blames Raymond Burr and Erle Stanley Gardner for the way I turned out. As portrayed by Burr, Perry Mason was a criminal defense lawyer. I loved how, during the trial, Perry always got the guilty party to confess on the stand. On the TV show, Mr. Mason got his 'not guilty' verdict in less than five minutes. If only that were the case in real life!

Suffice it to say that Coco Chanel, John Molloy and Perry Mason would all have found themselves on the back foot in an Arkansas courtroom ... or in my first law office, for that matter. When I began practicing, I could only afford a part-time secretary. For much of the day, I was alone in the office, and people walking in often assumed *I* was the secretary. That's natural, I suppose, but I tired of their mistake rather quickly.

In actuality, running a law office was nothing like the Perry Mason episodes I'd watched so assiduously. Whatever case was featured on that particular week's show seemed to be the only case Mr. Mason and Della, his Girl Friday, had to worry about. In the real world, however, a good attorney often has so many cases that even efficient office staff members find it hard to keep them all straight.

Sometimes, the jury in a civil or criminal case takes days or even weeks to come back with a verdict: Guilty, not guilty or a hung jury. The longest time I had to wait for a verdict was five hours. Let me tell you: Those hours of waiting had me biting my nails. At one point, the stress of waiting and wondering caused me to develop an eye tic!

My law school instructors never told me that, as an attorney, I would spend copious amounts of time waiting. But wait I did! I waited for the judge to call my case. I waited for the opposing lawyer to return my calls. And I always waited on pins and needles for the jury to come back with a verdict.

My first civil jury trial was an accident case. Civil cases cover everything that is not a criminal case. Criminal cases, of course, are typically tried by the State or federal government, represented by the local prosecuting attorney or district attorney. In civil cases, on the other hand, there are no criminal penalties. Usually, all the plaintiff wants is money for out-of-pocket damages including medical bills, pain and suffering, loss of consortium and other monetary losses.

The lawyer gets the biggest fee for the pain and suffering the client incurs. My first-year torts professor revealed the value of being paid money for permanent, often excruciating pain suffered by the plaintiff. As I remember, the professor asked: "How much money would you take in exchange for your thumb?"

"Which thumb?" some students asked.

"Right or left thumb?" I wondered.

The young man sitting beside me muttered that he was left-handed, in case that made a difference.

"Either thumb," the instructor responded.

One female law student timidly raised her hand. "One million dollars," she said. That was a lot of money in 1979.

The professor hastily added that the procedure of removing the thumb would be paid for, and—for what it was worth—also relatively painless. Of course, any thinking person knows that having your thumb cut off hurts. The amputation site will hurt while healing after surgery, and you often experience 'phantom pain' for the rest of your life.

"Would you be given hydrocodone, Percocet or another opiate in copious amounts to deal with the pain in your swollen, now-thumbless hand?" I inquired. The class forged ahead on that line of thought.

"How much would you take to sell your right leg?" the professor asked.

A rather arrogant male student said he'd take $5 million, and then he turned bright red, as if telling us his price was akin to admitting original sin.

"Okay," said my professor, "think about being on crutches, or in a walker, or in a wheelchair for six to eight months before you have your prosthetic device fitted … hopefully, by a competent professional." The instructor was creating a pretty vivid image of pain and suffering, which made human misery hard to discount and almost impossible to ignore.

Another female student said she would not sell thumb, leg or any other appendage to anyone. The whole class cheered her to the echo. If you can't imagine law school being an exciting place, take heart; this was a rare occurrence.

Of course, the whole point of the exercise was to point out that you can never be fully compensated for emotional distress and pain and suffering following the sudden loss of an eye, the loss of a limb, and so on. No matter the amount, the remedy of money to the plaintiff is never really sufficient.

Anyway, my first case involved a chiropractor. There are two rules I tell people who are in accidents: Go straight to the Emergency Room. Do not pass go or collect $200.

Second, even if you're not really hurt, go to your family doctor or an emergency clinic and see a 'real' medical doctor. At the very least, see an osteopath. Do not see a physical therapist, a chiropractor or a voodoo practitioner unless you are referred to them by a medical doctor.

Candidly, this means you have to be careful, since some professionals can have a doctorate after their name. A counselor, for example, can be Dr. Paine rather than Mr. Paine.

My client, Bill, had a really good friend who was a chiropractor. Bill was driving his little Toyota Camry when he was hit by an SUV. As a result of the accident, Bill was in a good deal of pain; his neck and back were killing him.

Instead of following the rules, however, Bill waited two days and then decided to go see his chiropractor friend. This is always a red-flag event; the chiropractor is *not* a medical doctor. The situation was complicated by the fact that the chiropractor was also Bill's close friend. Both are no-nos under the law.

Of course, the chiropractor adjusted Bill's neck and back. Bill had been rear-ended, and the collision had precipitated acute muscle strain in Bill's entire neck and back. Bill was in really sad shape, compounded by the fact that the chiropractor did not prescribe pain relievers or muscle relaxers. A competent medical doctor would have prescribed both.

Chiropractic regimen being what it is, the treatment Bill received did not include a single FDA prescription. Instead, Bill took copious amounts of extra strength Tylenol. The end result was that he continued to suffer. Bill's torment brought my law school class vividly to mind.

At length, we had an exciting one-day jury trial. The attorneys started at 9 o'clock in the morning, picked the dozen jurors, and the whole kit and caboodle was completed by 5 o'clock the same afternoon. The jury was out just over an hour. The verdict was for the plaintiff; we had won, or so I thought. The money was the rub: Bill was only awarded $5000 for chiropractic bills and $2000 for pain and suffering. Since I never took my fee out of awarded medical expenses, that meant my contingency fee was a third of $2000, or a whopping $666.

Because there was no medical consultation with a medical doctor, and because only a chiropractor was involved in treating Bill, the jury awarded only $7000. In my view, the jury might as well have offered nothing at all.

Perry Mason might have done better, but with an Arkansas jury, I doubt it. After the fiasco with Bill, I learned to take accident cases in which the plaintiffs had been seriously injured. There also had to be some good insurance on the other side to pay for the damages!

Accident cases were nothing if not unique. One crisp fall morning, Joe and Bertha were driving to Morrilton, a town about 25 miles east of Russellville. The elderly couple were headed back to their small country home. A young man hit Joe's car, forcing the automobile to careen into a deep ditch. Bertha was killed instantly. Joe sustained some cuts and whiplash. They had been married 60-odd years; both were in their 80s.

Joe hired me to represent him. He had a rather prickly demeanor, as many elderly gentlemen tend to have. I was patient and listened to Joe, who was tormented by grief. Bertha's sudden death had left him bereft.

I took the case on a contingency basis, so that if I did not win, I didn't earn a dime. The opposing counsel was Sam, a hard-bitten Little Rock attorney who was then in his 80s. His client was a thirty-something young man.

The notion of an octogenarian still practicing law required some effort to reconcile. The plain truth was that Sam was still making alimony payments to a spate of ex-wives, and couldn't retire. How his greasy vagabond of a client landed upon Sam, of all the lawyers out there, is still something of a mystery to me.

As a defense attorney, Sam would normally have argued that Bertha, at 83 years old, had already exceeded the life expectancy of a woman and that her husband therefore wasn't entitled to much in the way of compensation for Bertha's death. Of course, Sam himself would be living proof that this argument was a fallacy, and I was prepared to take full advantage of the fact that Sam was sitting in the courtroom with us, still practicing law.

As the trial date drew nigh, however, Sam decided to settle. When a civil case is settled, only the attorneys and parties know the amount of money involved. We received the maximum payout from the defendant's auto insurance and from Joe's insurance policies as well. Of course, the money could not absolve Joe of grief; his wife, with whom he had spent decades, was gone. No amount of money could bring Bertha back.

I did some aggressive advertising to solicit accident cases. When I went to law school in 1979, I moved to San Diego. Life in California was a culture shock, to say the least. One of the things that was hard for me to accept was how far ahead California was in many things, including the law. To me, California laws seemed about a decade ahead of the south and midwest.

From the 1960s on, the California Supreme Court enacted something called 'judicial legislation.' The court would create torts like 'intentional infliction of emotional distress.' This tort occurred when someone caused extreme emotional upset to another, and did so intentionally rather than by accident. An example might be a person driving drunk and running into a freestanding telephone booth in which someone happened to be making a call.

That situation actually happened, believe it or not. In that era, there were still public phone booths on almost every corner, and the case arose when a man in a phone booth, making a phone call, was run down. To add insult to serious injury, the man's wife was actually watching as a truck plowed into the phone booth. The man went to the hospital with serious injuries, including a broken leg and broken ribs. The wife understandably suffered shock and emotional distress.

This particular wreck was ruled intentional, and in an intentional tort, the plaintiff receives treble damages, or three times the amount of the judgment. I was amazed at how the California Supreme Court effectively made law with this case. Of course, the laws of a particular State are usually determined by that State's legislature. The audacious California Supreme Court made the law instead.

When I was in law school, California attorneys were advertising on television and virtually every other medium as well. When I returned to Arkansas in 1983, there was very little advertising being done by local attorneys. I knew I had to advertise, so I contacted a Yellow Pages representative. I was one of the first attorneys to use my own photo in a Yellow Pages ad. Being the only local 'lady lawyer,' my photo tended to stand out, and I got a lot of calls because people wanted a female advocate. As if on cue, my male colleagues then started putting their own photos in their ads.

I myself was involved in an accident that was litigated. I live on a curvy country road that leads up to a State highway. Coming off the highway and down my road, there's a blind curve. Bamboo was growing high enough that drivers could not see around the curve. As I took Kane to school one morning, I was unable to see around the curve at all. As we drove around the corner, there was a huge yellow school bus lumbering down the incline from the highway. I managed to pull all the way off the road and stop. I waited for the Dover school bus to hit me, and it did. The front fender rammed into the back of my little Nissan Altima.

Kane and I were not injured. The bus driver got out and came to see if we were okay. All the students on the bus and the driver were unhurt, except for one girl who claimed that she'd hit her hand on the top of a school bus seat. A cyst on the hand resulted. A local attorney filed a lawsuit against the Dover school district and me. I was outraged. I reacted quickly enough to stop and pull over, after all, and I could not understand how I'd been negligent when the school bus hit *me*.

My insurance company and the other insurers settled with the student for a total of $2000—$1000 from each defendant. My ego was bruised, but the outcome worked out well. Kane and I hadn't been hurt, and my car was repaired.

When Sadie came to see me; I'd just gotten her guardianship, or custody, of her two grandsons. Their parents neglected them and were not caring for the boys properly. Not long afterwards, Sadie had been in a car accident in which she suffered whiplash and a chest injury caused by an exploding air bag. At least she was alone and the children were not with her! She went by ambulance to the hospital, and X-rays were taken. There was no injury to Sadie's spine; just muscle strain. Whiplash is quite traumatic, causing headaches and a good deal of pain. I tried to get a decent settlement so there would be no need for a trial. The amount that the insurance company was willing to pay was substantially less than Sadie had expected. Incidentally, the television ads for attorneys give folks incredibly wrong ideas about the huge settlements they'll receive if they suffer from another driver's negligence.

As it happened, my son had been a great Pokemon card collector. After Kane died, I wound up with a large collection of Pokemon cards. Sadie wanted a starter deck of Pokemon cards so her grandsons could play the Pokemon game. I made a deal with her: Take the settlement being offered, and I'll give you a trash bag full of Kane's Pokemon cards as part of the settlement. I reduced my fee as well, so Sadie was satisfied with the result.

One of Arkansas' moving vehicle laws prohibits backing up on a road or highway. Connie was coming down the highway near my home en route to a local recreational spot. Suddenly, a stopped truck began to back up the hill toward her. Connie was headed down the hill and could not stop in time; she ran into the bumper of the truck. Connie sustained whiplash and her airbags were deployed. When the airbags went off, it appeared that smoke was coming from the car. In reality, the smoke was a plume of caustic chemicals.

Connie suffered from headaches for several weeks. Even though she was in pain, Connie got out to check on the other driver. The truck driver was uninjured. Since he had violated a law, he was found negligent. We settled the case for medical bills, pain and suffering, and the value of Connie's car, which was totaled. She seemed pleased with the settlement.

One of my more exciting accident cases involved a rather large cow. A young woman, Rebecca, was driving down the highway. She was not speeding. Suddenly, this huge bovine lumbered out in front of her. Rebecca was in a red Corvette. The resulting impact with the cow smashed the hood and broke the windshield. Only by the grace of God was Rebecca not hurt. She just sustained property damage to her automobile. In case you're wondering, the cow was injured but survived.

First, I had to investigate who owned the cow. Second, I had to prove that the cow had gotten out before or that there was damage to the fence. This would have proven negligence on the owner's part. Locating the owner proved to be no real difficulty.

The attorney representing the owner was older and more experienced. Richard Peel assumed I would be so 'green' that he could easily win the case for his client, who was a local barber. The defendant, I discovered, had left a defective fence in place. His cows were often out in the road, causing a public nuisance. We had a court trial heard by a judge since both sides had waived a jury trial.

I had tried criminal jury cases, but two are like apples and oranges. A non-jury trial was a picnic in comparison. A jury trial, whether civil or criminal, is very stressful and represents rather a lot of work. With a non-jury trial, on the other hand, you don't have to worry about a rogue juror going off the rails and finding for the other side.

My trial in front of the judge went well. I proved negligence. Specifically, I proved that the defendant's cows were often out in the road. I also proved damages, which were about $5000. That represented the amount of the damage to Rebecca's Corvette. She had not been seriously hurt, but if she had hit a cow head-on, she would have been killed. She and I were very happy with the outcome; I've often wondered what sort of excuses Richard Peel made to his client!

A short time later, the defendant told me that the cows in question actually belonged to the defendant's brother. He'd paid the damages rather than betray his sibling.

In another accident case, a woman stopped her car and a huge truck ran into her. The impact was akin to a bowling ball striking a golf ball. The sheer force of the collision jostled my client's brain, resulting in a loss of memory and headaches and neck pain. My client was driving through a construction zone and had stopped for a flagman; unfortunately, the truck behind her did not stop. I was able to settle the case for a fair sum of money.

I took a wrongful death case. Trudy came to see me following an fatality that was due to the negligence of another party. Her husband, Frank, died in the accident. An 18-wheeler carrying Bob's Whirl-A-Twirl, an amusement ride with protruding arms, passed my client's 18-wheeler on the Interstate. One of the ride's arms came through the driver's window, beheading my client's husband. His wife, sitting next to him, was unhurt.

I wound up referring the case out to a large Little Rock law firm. I received a quarter of the attorney's fee for sending the client their way. This fee was probably the easiest fee I ever earned as an attorney.

Following one particular property line dispute case, I never practiced property law again. My client was a sweet little old lady. In law school, they taught us that the most sympathetic client to have was a proverbial little old lady in tennis shoes.

Unfortunately, Mildred had serious heart problems. Her own grandson had sued her over a property line dispute; the difference was just a couple of feet. Of course, being sued by her grandson caused Mildred a good deal of emotional stress, which is always a challenge for a cardiac patient.

Thankfully, I settled the property line dispute without a deposition from Mildred. The case did not go to trial. Mildred was, as we say in lawyer parlance, a 'satisfied customer.'

I never took a single slander or libel case, never took a slip and fall case, and never practiced patent or copyright law. I never represented the big banks or insurance companies against a plaintiff. I had little respect for *any* attorney who was paid by an insurance company to defend a case. I called these folks 'insurance defense attorneys,' which is what they are. They somehow manage to get paid whether they win or lose. If an insurance company hires an outside attorney, you can bet that the lawyer is being paid by the hour regardless of the outcome of the matter in question.

I always tried to ensure that my clients received more money than I did. Of course, that's not often the case in the legal world; attorneys sometimes take a third to 40% from an accident settlement. Charging the fees I charged, I guess that's why I didn't get rich as an attorney. For example, if I received a $50,000 settlement award, I always made sure each accident client got more of the settlement amount than I did.

The main job of these 'insurance defense attorneys' is to keep a plaintiff who had been seriously injured or neglected—neglected, say, in a nursing home—from recovering a fair amount of money as compensation. In civil cases, I was always representing the plaintiff. I often said that I represented a number of 'street people.' I literally pulled them from ditches. But I could sleep well at night because I had a clean conscience. I was serving God by practicing law.

Of course, I was a 'street person' myself . . . but not in the way you think. Over the years, most of my offices were very near the county courthouse, which meant that I could walk to court. The courthouse was, at most, only a few blocks away from my office. Since I had 'Walker' in my name, folks called me "The Street Walker." I guess that was funnier to some than others.

Another area of civil law involves class action suits. As an example, I helped a client with class action suit. My secretary's husband was in the class against his employer, Con Agra, a food processing facility in Russellville. The case focused on workers and the time they took donning and doffing safety equipment and coveralls before and after work. In all, donning and doffing took workers about 40 minutes per day, for which they received no pay. The class action suit asked for pay for time spent donning and doffing clothing and equipment. The firm that filed the class action suit worked with my office.

Unfortunately, the court ruled that the workers did not get paid for the time it took to don and doff their apparel. This case was appealed, but the higher court affirmed the decision. Not a single class action lawsuit participant got a red cent from Con Agra. In fact, the law office that filed the suit against Con Agra barely made anything from all the work they'd done on the case.

I never filed my own class action lawsuit because I always had a small law practice. Just the cost of mailing documents to each plaintiff in a class action lawsuit is exorbitant. In a typical law firm, you might need two or three attorneys to file and complete a class action suit.

On the other hand, I love to be a member of class action suits. Over the years, I've received checks from various companies because I joined a class action suit. My stepson was always signing up for class action suits, and he often had a nice income stream as a result.

As I finished law school, I fully intended to go to Anchorage, Alaska with my friend, Rebecca, who hailed from there. Since there were no Alaskan law schools to attend, Rebecca had come to the University of San Diego, and we'd met. What stopped me from moving to Alaska? First, the period of total darkness in winter, and second, the vast geographic distance from Arkansas where my parents and sister lived dissuaded me as well. Flying back home from Alaska would be cost-prohibitive, especially for a neophyte lawyer.

Instead, I remained in San Diego and took the California Bar. The pass rate was only about 30 percent. Along with New York, California has the most difficult Bar exam in the United States. I never regretted taking the Bar in California, but—since I remained in Arkansas—I never used my California license. My law school instructors had prepared me to be a decent attorney.

The problem with staying in San Diego was that a tiny shack cost over $100,000. Buying a home or property was therefore cost-prohibitive. In Arkansas, back then, I could practically buy a mansion for $100,000. I had already gone into debt—over $40,000—to attend USD. Private law schools are always expensive. I could have bought a nice three-bedroom home in Arkansas for the same amount! I paid off my student debt within a decade, and never regretted leaving California to come home.

Over the years, I discovered that I needed a therapist's skills to help my clients with depression and anxiety issues. Some were even paranoid schizophrenics. If I sat and talked with a schizophrenic person for a long period of time, they began to make sense!

Counseling someone without appropriate training was something of a slippery slope. I finally realized some clients just needed me to listen about how badly their spouse had treated them or about the problems their children were having. I took a deep breath and let their stories spill out. I remember it was very difficult not to interrupt and ask questions. I needed facts to represent them, of course, in order to provide guidance and legal advice. But facts were, quite often, the last thing forthcoming from talkative clients.

Sometimes, a client would telephone me without an appointment. I would ask how I could help. "Ms. Walker," the client responded, "I just needed to hear your voice." To paraphrase Bob Marley, the client needed reassurance that every little thing would be okay.

Attorneys are called 'counselors at law.' One of my best traits as an attorney was the ability to sit and listen to a client weep or talk nonstop. I often wished I'd gotten a psychology degree so I could have better counseled clients. The 'counseling' aspect of my work gave me great satisfaction; I honestly felt I was serving the very people that God had put me on this earth to help. I treated everyone the same, regardless of how rich or poor they were, the color of their skin, their religion, or background. Even my poorest clients often went out of their way to thank me. They baked me cookies, hugged me, and became my dear friends.

The values of respect and treating others as I would want to be treated, absorbed from going to church for 30 years, became my law office mantra. I took the Biblical injunction to 'love thy neighbor' quite seriously. For that reason, I reckon, I never became wealthy practicing law.

When I closed my office in 2020, I told friends that the only aspects of law practice I would miss would be my clients and my secretary, and time has proven me right. From time to time, however, I still watch Perry Mason reruns.

CHAPTER SIX

The Wheels of Justice

In the summer of 1984, I hung up my shingle and opened my law office. Like most neophyte attorneys, however, I had no practical experience. My degree in Elementary Education didn't prove to be of much benefit. At that point, I didn't even know how to draft a will or a divorce complaint. Almost immediately, I needed serious help.

My rescuer was an unlikely father-figure—my 8th grade Sunday School teacher at First United Methodist Church. Doc Irwin was an attorney; he was also a kind man with big heart. During my first couple of years in practice, I would stop by his office to learn how to draft a complaint to start a case. There would always be a dozen other people sitting in his waiting room, waiting their turn to talk to Doc. Doc practiced law solo. I've always been grateful that he in would take time out of his day to guide me in the practice of law.

Of Doc's seven children, three became attorneys. Doc was truly amazing to observe in court, largely because he was an old country attorney. He used bad grammar, like, "He don't know what is good for him. Only his attorney does." Doc just shot from the hip and typically won the case. In my 36 years practicing law, Doc was the finest trial attorney I ever saw.

Doc handled mostly criminal jury trials and contested divorces. He could spin a story that would mesmerize a dozen jurors. At some point, Doc started taking on bankruptcy cases to try to avoid handling so many divorces, but the change of specialties didn't help much. Pathetic, desperate women still wanted Doc Irwin to handle their divorces, and he did.

Whatever else he might have been, Doc was also a masterful juggler. He would appear in court in Russellville and tell the judge that he had to be in court in Morrilton. In a word, Doc was supposed to be somewhere else all the time. Doc needed to split, like an amoeba.

I was at a docket call in criminal court one day and watched our deputy prosecutor working over a poor, unrepresented man. Doc strode up to the bench. "I represent Joe," he told the judge. "Let me take him out into the hall and we can settle this matter." Doc disappeared with the man, who hadn't paid Doc a dime. In no time, Doc and his new client had worked out a brilliant plea agreement with the deputy prosecutor. Whenever I think of Doc Irwin these days, I think of a man with an extraordinarily large heart. He inspired me to be a better attorney.

Just because I was a lady lawyer, that didn't mean I had much in common with other lady lawyers. Doc Irwin had seven children. Three of them—John, Seth and Nancy—also became lawyers. Nancy Irwin was one of the most delightful members of the Pope County Bar Association. She was somewhat younger than me, but she had a sparkle in her eyes ... just like Doc. We became friends and always tried to settle cases without recourse to the courtroom. We often had lunch; I discovered that, like her father, she was smart and helpful. I was somewhat distraught when she moved away to northwest Arkansas.

Dale Finley was another inspiration. Dale was our juvenile judge; he was also a very capable attorney. I learned much just going to his court when I was appointed or hired to represent juvenile delinquents. I remember one afternoon when I was writing a custody case brief for Judge Mobley, and I welcomed the interruption when my secretary buzzed to tell me Dale Finley was in the waiting room, reading a magazine. Dale had come to my office to escape his own, or perhaps he was hiding from a client ... I don't know which.

Dale's partner was Jim Young, an older attorney. To say that their partnership had created a chaotic office environment was something of an understatement. A quiet man, Dale put a high value on peace and tranquility, and he often said he enjoyed both those things in my small office. I spent a good deal of time at Dale's office as well, with Dale helping me complete the paperwork for a Chapter 7 bankruptcy. In Chapter 7, the debtor discharges all of their debts, unless they want to reaffirm a debt. Many times, the debtor in question would reaffirm their automobile, which allowed them to keep their means of transportation. The payments continued, of course.

Chapter 13 bankruptcies were something I chose not to handle. In a Chapter 13, the debtor reorganized their debts and assets and paid 60% to 80% of the debt. Assets were subject to return; if you gave back your washer and dryer, that effectively cancelled your debt. Many debtors found a way to pay off their physician so they could keep seeing their doctor. When the bankruptcy code changed some years later, the new requirements stipulated that a bankruptcy had to be filed via computer in a Federal court. At that point, I stopped taking bankruptcy cases.

Dale Finley was a huge help when I had to write a Petition for Habeas Corpus or a petition to increase Child Support. "Susan," he'd tell me, "just specify in the petition the relief you're requesting." If, for example, I was writing a petition to increase Child Support, I would mention that circumstances had changed for the non-custodial parent—usually the father—and that he should pay more in Child Support since his net income had increased. When Dale talked me through the process, it all made sense.

For my first dozen years in practice, I represented individuals charged with felony drug violations. These individuals were charged with selling cocaine or methamphetamines. I finally quit handling felony law altogether because I didn't want to be retained with dirty drug money.

The difference between a felony and a misdemeanor is significant: A felony conviction earns the guilty party time in prison in addition to a fine or restitution to the victim. As an example, a class 'C' felony typically carries a prison sentence ranging from three to ten years and up to a $10,000 fine.

The defendant must always pay restitution. In a battery case, for example, where the defendant badly injures the victim, the defendant would be required to pay the victim's medical bills as restitution. A misdemeanor offense carries a sentence of up to a year in county jail and a $1,000 fine. Sometimes, as was the case with DWI convictions, the fines might be substantially larger.

I learned to avoid jury trials at all cost. I always tried to work out a deal with the prosecutor to avoid trying a case.

Our local Holiday Inn was the setting for one of my more benign felony cases. The hotel kept its trash near the highway, behind a wooden privacy fence. One day, Holiday Inn employees headed to Blackwell, just across the Pope County line, to purchase liquor for the hotel's private club. They drove a van and removed the back seat from the vehicle so they might transport more alcohol.

The van seat was left outside the privacy fence, in plain view to motorists heading up and down the highway. My client and his brother were driving by, spotted the abandoned seat, and stopped to pick up their roadside booty. The two men placed the seat in their vehicle and drove off.

Russellville police arrested my client for theft by receiving. The charge was that my client had stolen the van seat and still had it in his possession. In this particular case, we actually went ahead to a jury trial. My not-so-bright client testified that he believed the van seat had been abandoned as trash. The jury came back with a verdict of not guilty. I began to think that maybe jury trials weren't so bad after all.

This was a miscalculation on my part. Since we had no public defender in my county, and I was the only 'lady lawyer' in the area, I was often appointed to represent the rather unsavory defendants charged in felony cases. One of those individuals was a convicted felon named Kenny Hamm. Kenny and his friend had the bright idea to rob local used car salesman Cowboy Ferguson, who almost always kept $6000 to $8000 in cash in his wallet. Kenny was the getaway driver; his friend robbed Cowboy and used a gun for the purpose. The use of a firearm made this robbery an enhanced felony.

As soon as Kenny was arrested, he sang like a canary. The physical evidence made it a solid-enough case. Usually, I received cases like this after defendant was already in custody and had confessed to the crime. At Kenny's one-day trial, the prosecutor introduced Kenny's confession and had an officer read it to jury. This was a clear violation of the best evidence rule. Russellville police officers had recorded Kenny's confession on a cassette tape, transcribed the tape, and then reused it. There was no way to determine if the confession transcript was accurate.

Kenny was convicted, but I appealed the verdict to the Arkansas Supreme Court. I went in front of the justices in Little Rock and argued the case. The high court ruled that because the Russellville Police Department hadn't been prudent enough to save the original cassette tape, the transcript of Kenny's confession could not be admitted as evidence. In court, the officer had read the confession to the jury via a transcript. The Supreme Court ruled this was a reversible error, and the case was reversed and remanded for retrial.

During the appeal process, of course, Kenny was serving time. On the day of the preliminary hearing, a sheriff's deputy brought Kenny back from prison in a prison grey uniform. If Kenny was happy to be out of custody for the day, he didn't look it. Instead of being grateful for new trial, as I expected he would be, the defendant was actually quite angry with me.

At the time, I was about five months pregnant, and my condition was obvious. During the conference, Kenny threatened to kill me. I presumed he was also threatening to kill my baby. I told the trial judge I needed to be relieved as counsel. The judge made short shrift of my request, probably due to the fact that I had appealed the original guilty verdict.

"Too bad," the judge said, and banged his gavel.

My partner David took over the case. The judge's decision was not a monumental tragedy, since I had been appointed to defend Kenny and our firm was making peanuts for the effort. David had to retry the case; this time, Kenny received a sentence of 40 years in prison.

My mantra: The wheels of justice grind slowly, if at all.

Here's a question for you: How do you win a suppression hearing without saying a word? The little incident I'm about to recount actually started when I fell ill with a virus; I wound up losing my voice. I couldn't make a sound. Of course, most people like it when an attorney loses her voice; I felt my husband enjoyed the peace and quiet in our home.

Unfortunately, I had a suppression hearing set for two days later. My client, Joe, was charged with Possession of a Controlled Substance With Intent To Deliver. The police officers had a search warrant for Joe's home. The warrant allowed for a search for weapons, especially guns.

Luckily for Joe, the officers could find no guns. However, there was a small cabinet that had very little drawers. The drawers were far too small for any type of gun to fit within. The deputy opened five of the little drawers and found cocaine in two of them. Joe was arrested for Possession of a Controlled Substance With Intent to Deliver.

The day of the hearing arrived. I had prayed mightily the night before that my voice might be restored, but I awoke with absolutely no voice. As I drove to the hearing that morning, I was hoping that the judge would grant me a continuance to allow me to retain my ability to speak.

As things worked out, I was standing in front of Judge Eddy and I was literally speechless. A few minutes before court began, I wrote a note to the deputy Prosecuting Attorney. It read:

> *I have no voice. If I write my questions out to you, will you be my mouthpiece today?*

Ken Helton, a good lawyer and my friend, nodded yes, so I had it made. A week or so before the hearing, I had written down all of questions I wanted to ask the two deputies from the Yell County Sheriff's Office. I calmly handed my questions to Ken, and he blinked—twice. He realized that I had some hard questions for the deputies.

In the hearing, I had the burden of proving that the 4th Amendment had been violated, and that the discovery of cocaine should be suppressed. Since Joe's possession of cocaine was the only evidence of the crime, my client would be freed if I won the motion. The deputies admitted that no firearm could have been jammed into the little drawers. There was just a small amount of cocaine in each drawer. The judge with the snowy white hair and kind blue eyes looked down at Ken, Joe and me. "For being unable to say a word, Ms. Allen, you presented some fine arguments. If the State has no additional evidence, I'm going to dismiss the case."

Ken said, "We have no other evidence, Your Honor."

The judge banged his gavel, and the case was dismissed. I was pretty proud of myself for winning the case, especially considering I had never said a word.

Another rather complicated felony case to which I was appointed involved attempted murder, kidnapping, rape, and felony battery. I was appointed by a judge to represent Lonnie Mitchell. Lonnie was a young black man, tall and sinewy. He had short hair, brown eyes, and mocha-colored skin, and was rather attractive.

Here are the facts: The victim, a young woman, got into Lonnie's car around midnight. Lonnie drove her to a quiet area ... a cul-de-sac in a new subdivision. From the way the young woman was behaving, Lonnie thought she wanted to make out. She was an attractive blonde, with blue eyes.

The young lady became scared quite suddenly, and she got out of the car. She made the mistake of using a racial slur. Lonnie beat the young woman to a pulp and then raped her.

When the victim took the stand at Lonnie's trial, her wounds had healed. She had no permanent damage to her appearance. That, in and of itself, was something of a miracle. Succinctly, she told the jury that Lonnie had stomped her face with his tennis shoe and then raped her. Lonnie's tennis shoe left a pattern on her bruised cheek; the bruise matched the tread of tennis shoe. Russellville police officers searched Lonnie's bedroom; he lived with his grandparents and they had given their consent to the search. The officers found Lonnie's bloody tennis shoes and other physical evidence.

Of course, Lonnie confessed. I could not exclude the confession, and the case appeared open and shut. We needed an entire day to select the jury, and two days for the trial. Lonnie was found guilty and given two life sentences, plus 30 years. The prison terms were to be served consecutively.

The only problem here was jury pool. There was just one black person in the pool. With a preemptory challenge, prosecutor John Bynum excused the black gentleman without cause. This left an all-white jury. Unfortunately for Mr. Bynum, the Arkansas Supreme Court cited his juror dismissal as a reversible error when I appealed the verdict. In *Baston V. Kentucky,* a 1986 U. S. Supreme Court decision, the high court ruled that prosecutors could not preemptively challenge all jurors of same race as defendant. Minority jurors could only be excused for cause if their dismissal left you with all-white jury.

Bynum's mistake was using a peremptory challenge to excuse the only black juror in the jury pool. The Arkansas Supreme Court reversed the verdict and remanded the case for retrial. However, the judge was not happy about re-trying the case; he had a very busy and demanding trial docket. If felony charges were not tried in a timely manner, the Speedy Trial rule attached and all charges would be dropped. The defendant would be freed.

The retrial took another three days. This time, Lonnie received two life sentences *and* 40 years, to be served consecutively.

I had much better luck with a defendant who had been charged with five burglaries and thefts. I was appointed because the defendant was indigent; he could not bond out. Once again, John Bynum was the prosecutor. Since the defendant was incarcerated, Bynum had nine months in which to try the case. The nine months ran their course, and the already-convicted felon was released and all charges dropped for violation of the Speedy Trial rule. Bynum had let a convicted felon walk free.

At that point, I had a rather heated conversation with the Sheriff of nearby Johnson County. The Sheriff took umbrage because the defendant had been freed on what the Sheriff considered a "minor technicality." Of course, it is the prosecutor's job to keep track of time and avoid having such charges dismissed. The Speedy Trial rule is a cruel timekeeper. I felt no guilt whatsoever; in no way was Bynum's oversight a "minor technicality." Whenever such charges are summarily dismissed because the State has abused the time-frame, the prosecutor must take the blame for the mistake.

I tried a single felony case in Federal Court in Little Rock. A tall black man matching my client's description had robbed a Russellville bank. My client was in the Pope County Detention Center waiting for a trial. Because Russellville is in the Eastern division of the State, the courthouse of jurisdiction is in Little Rock. Bank robbery is a Federal crime.

To commit the robbery, the bandit had dressed as a UPS driver and pulled a gun once inside the bank. The use of the gun made this an enhanced felony. I don't remember how much money was stolen, but it wasn't enough to justify the sentence my client received.

I had to drive 100 miles to Little Rock and be in court before 9am. Selection of the jury went quickly compared to a State case. The trial lasted a single long day. My client did not take the stand, and he had no alibi. The jury returned quickly, and rendered a verdict of guilty. Because a gun was involved, my client was sentenced to life in prison.

My client had left his personal property in a rental car. As he sat in jail, he asked me to retrieve his basketball, clothing and other items from the trunk of the rental. I obliged and stored his property in my office attic. One of my client's family members was supposed to come and retrieve my client's property, but no one ever showed up.

Several months after the trial, I was served with a subpoena *duces tecum,* which required me to hand over the brown UPS uniform and clipboard that were part of my client's personal property. With a Federal Marshall in my office, I had no choice but to comply immediately. The man watched every move I made. I was now squarely in the middle of the chain of custody of the clothing and clipboard my client had used in the bank robbery.

The ensuing events added insult to injury. I was subpoenaed to Federal court in Birmingham, Alabama for an additional robbery trial. I had to testify as to the chain of custody of the fake UPS uniform. My former client glared at me while I was on the stand. Convicted of a second robbery as well, my client went back to Federal prison.

A few months later, I was subpoenaed to testify at a third bank robbery trial. This time, I had to go to Memphis, Tennessee. My former client was less than excited to see me and gave me scathing looks as I testified about the chain of custody. Incidentally, my former client had no type of badge or other identification as a UPS driver ... he just had the brown uniform everyone associates with a UPS employee.

When you are a witness in Federal court, they pay you well for mileage to and from court. I also had a nice per diem and stayed in beautiful hotels. In both cities, I could literally walk to the trial. Downtown Memphis was a bit scary, but I emerged from the experience unscathed.

I took two things away from this experience: First, I took no more Federal felony cases, and second, I never again took possession of a client's personal property.

After I had Kane, I stopped going to Federal court because I had to drive 100 miles to Little Rock or 90 miles to Fort Smith. I was gone from early in the morning until late at night. With a young child at home, I wanted to be closer to Russellville. I gave up the 'big money' and resolved to stay well within a 50-mile distance from Russellville. Ozark and Paris, Arkansas marked the western edge of my purview. I effectively altered my law practice so I could be closer to home in case my son needed me.

Russellville was never a boring place ... at least, not for very long. I remember being retained to defend Anna, who was charged with theft. This white-collar crime occurred when Anna worked for Friendship Services, a local organization that has long served the mentally handicapped. Anna was handling client money in client accounts. The Friendship clients received monthly Supplemental Security Income—SSI—checks. In turn, Friendship would give clients $30 to $50 a month for spending money.

Anna thought up a clever plan to abscond with some of the money from these client accounts. She wrote small checks that she herself cashed. The prosecutor could only prove she stole over

$30,000 from clients. The prosecutor felt Anna had stolen more, but he could not prove it. Anna was convicted in a jury trial.

Remember that everyone is presumed innocent until proven guilty in court. As an attorney, I drew more flack over my defense of Anna than any other case. "How can you represent people you know are guilty?" the townspeople often asked. I took the time to explain that every defendant in a criminal trial has the right to zealous and competent representation, regardless of whether they are guilty or innocent. I felt no guilt when working out a plea or trying to strike the best deal possible when someone had *confessed* to a crime. Anna didn't confess.

The Sixth Amendment to the United States Constitution states that every defendant is entitled to a competent attorney and a speedy trial, among other things. I grew tired of explaining to people that I was tasked with representing the defendant regardless of the situation. Local folks would often shake their heads and walk away in disgust.

Sir Thomas More once said to his son, "The currents and eddies of right and wrong that you find such plain sailing are, for me, impossible to navigate." I've reluctantly concluded that many members of jury pools believe themselves smarter than Sir Thomas.

Anna's jury trial proceeded with the full dozen jurors. I knew the jury foreperson, who was head engineer at nearby Arkansas Nuclear One. I made my usual zealous presentation of Anna's defense. Then the accountant for Friendship Services took the stand to testify about the amount of money Anna had stolen. After the CPA answered the prosecutor's questions, I had the opportunity to cross-examine him. I politely asked, "When was last time your client's accounts were audited?"

"Never," the CPA responded. A yearly audit would have been expected and might have protected the Friendship clients' accounts.

The jury did not take kindly to this lack of interest in protecting the individual accounts. Of course, they did find Anna guilty, but the jury hung on the sentencing phase. Some of the jurors wanted Anna to serve probation and no jail time. Other members of the panel wanted Anna to spend 7 years in prison.

Anna was sentenced to serve 2 years in the State penitentiary. She also had to pay around $45,000 in income tax and penalties on the money she stole, and she was required to restitute the Friendship clients. Not surprisingly, Anna's husband divorced her and I never heard from Anna again.

Nonetheless, I considered this a real win for me. For a time, my faith that juries will sometimes do the right thing was renewed.

John Bynum was a zealous prosecuting attorney. However, John tended to be a bit too strict on law-and-order issues. I had occasion to have a conference with Bynum about some cases I was trying to resolve. I was trying to arrange for a plea or get the prosecutor's office to dismiss what I considered to be a very weak case. I had been appointed to defend three individuals who had been charged with various crimes, and one case was so weak that it should have been dismissed.

I argued my position in the prosecutor's office. His response shocked me: "If the defendant didn't commit this crime," Bynum said, "he got away with others and should still go to prison, Susan. Don't be so goddamn stupid."

I stared at the prosecutor for a moment. I was dumbfounded; for once in my life, I was actually at a loss for words.

I put my files back in my briefcase, got up and marched out of John's office. My friends will tell you that it's hard to get me mad, but when I'm angry, rage blows through me like a tornado or a wild thunderstorm. I threw open Bynum's glass front door and slammed it shut. Thankfully, the glass did not break.

Whenever I think back to that case, I think back a few years further as well. I'd grown up in Russellville, and people knew me and my family. When I was deciding to return home to practice,

I canvassed the male lawyers to assess their attitude toward a lady in their midst.

"There are already enough attorneys in Russellville," John Bynum told me.

"But there are no *women* attorneys here," I replied.

Bynum mumbled something in reply, then changed the subject.

When those arrests and verdicts were vacated, I felt something akin to competitive pride … after all, I hadn't exactly been welcomed with open arms. What goes around does, indeed, come around.

I think it's pretty evident that I could never have been a prosecuting attorney or a state's attorney. I was Susan Walker Allen for the defense. Strangely, while I enjoyed reading criminal cases, the practice of criminal law—and clients involved—was more drama than I wanted to handle. That's why I stopped taking felony cases and handled only simple misdemeanors for rest of my years in practice.

The singular moral of this whole story: Crime does not pay. The law caught up with a young man who had robbed bank after bank. Anna thought she would get rich stealing from adults with special needs. Another young black man became irrationally angry when a victim used a racial slur. Yet another thought stopping at the side of the road to pick up a discarded van seat was a good idea.

As I noted, many people think law practice in a small town must be a slow and boring affair. To the contrary! I caught a wide gamut of cases while the ponderous wheels of justice ground their inexorable course.

CHAPTER SEVEN

A Misdemeanor

I WAS THE ONLY LADY LAWYER in my part of the state, and I meant business.

Paradoxically, I also *needed* business.

Under the Sixth Amendment, every citizen of the United States has the right to an attorney even if they cannot afford a lawyer. At that time, Pope County had no public defender, so local attorneys were appointed to defend indigent individuals charged with felonies or misdemeanors.

Guidelines helped judges determine whether the defendant was indigent. When they were, I was often appointed to defend them.

A misdemeanor offense, incidentally, carries a sentence of up to a year in the city jail, a fine, or both. One typical misdemeanor offense is shoplifting. I remember that I was appointed to represent Larry, a local man who found himself hungry while in a local grocery store. Larry slit open a package of hot dogs and took two to eat, leaving the other ten to be sold. Of course, store security caught him. Larry went to jail for several days before he could bond out.

When I met with Larry, I asked him why he didn't just take the whole pack of hot dogs. Larry explained that he was very hungry and had no money. He took the two hot dogs because taking the whole pack would be wrong.

Some people just need a stupid sign around their neck. Larry was one of these. We finally went to trial on the theft charge for stealing two hot dogs. Our Municipal Judge, Richard Peel—I called him 'King Richard'—fined Larry more than $250 in fines, court costs, and time served, which probably made those hot dogs among the most expensive Oscar Mayers ever consumed.

At that time, an entire pack of hot dogs cost less than $1. I was disgusted with the judge, because I was certain that the punishment did not fit the crime.

Several of my clients were charged with stealing two packs of cigarettes. In my experience, the most common item people shoplifted were two packs of cigarettes. They didn't steal one pack or four packs; they stole two packs every time. The stores finally figured this out for themselves and put all tobacco products behind glass. You had to request the cigarettes rather than steal them.

Cigarettes were notoriously expensive in the mid 1980s, and like many young women at the time, Cathy was addicted to nicotine. Of course, Cathy was convicted and had to pay both the fine and court costs … much more than it would have cost to buy two packs of cigarettes. I often went into these cases knowing that I would lose them; my job was to minimize the damage to my client.

I remember a particular shoplifting case that involved a woman I'll call Bunny. Bunny was 'shopping' at our local Walmart when she decided that she needed bigger breasts. While shopping in plain sight, Bunny stole breast enhancers and stuffed them into her bra. She was wearing a low-cut shirt and access to her bra wasn't a real problem.

Of course, the store security camera caught Bunny. She left the store without paying for the enhancers, and the police were called. Being a fast thinker, Bunny told police, "These are mine. I wore them in here." The problem was that the security camera had caught her in the act.

Bunny was arrested on Friday and spent three nights in jail before the municipal judge set her bond. She got time served for the three days she'd already spent in jail, and was fined more than

$500 for the theft. After the trial, I imagine Bunny either went out and bought breast enhancers or used bathroom tissue instead, like most of us girls did when we were young.

For whatever reason, I was appointed to represent people charged with DWI. I happen to be a teetotaler; I have never had more than half a glass of wine. I have only tasted beer, which reminded me of sour urine. Consequently, I don't exactly cotton to people who drink and drive, because they can easily kill themselves and others.

My client, Robert, had an obvious drinking problem. He was found passed out in his car, parked on the shoulder of Arkansas Highway 7 during the morning rush hour. The engine was turned off, but keys were still in the ignition. Even though Robert was sound asleep, the keys were within his reach. Robert was charged with Driving While Intoxicated. At that time, if you tested .10 blood alcohol content, you were charged with DWI.

Robert was sleeping peacefully when officers stopped to see why his car was parked in the left-hand lane of a four-lane road. Robert was obviously intoxicated, and he was taken to the Pope County Detention Center and given a breathalyzer test. He tested .39, even though the hour was still early morning. I remember being flatly amazed that Robert could test that high and still be conscious! He pled guilty in court, and was fined more than $600 in fines and costs.

The DWI case I remember most fondly was a client named Tom, who was weaving while driving and crossed the center line. An alert police officer stopped him and smelled alcohol. Tom was taken to the Detention Center, but he quickly bonded out. Back then, the bond wasn't much for DWI 1.

However, Tom couldn't afford an attorney. At that time, private attorneys charged $2000 retainer—or more—to represent a defendant charged with a first DWI. In fact, attorneys typically charged up to $5000 to represent clients charged with their second or third DWI.

By the time he arrived at the Detention Center, Tom was sober enough to refuse the breath test. Since he refused, he was charged with DWI and also something called Implied Consent. If a person was arrested for DWI or a successive DWI offense, the state had the right to compel them to take the breathalyzer test. If the arrested individual did not sign the consent form and take the test, they were automatically charged with Implied Consent. Implied Consent carried a six month suspension of the defendant's Driver's License.

After Tom bailed out, I met with him and asked why he'd refused the breath test. Tom told me that he had heard that if the police did not get a breath test from the defendant, it was easier to beat the DWI charge. Tom was totally correct; however, when you refuse the breath test, you are charged with Implied Consent. Your license should be automatically suspended for six months.

When you are convicted of DWI 1, your Driver's License is suspended for 90 days. You can get a work permit allowing you to drive to work and in emergencies. The work permit isn't available if you're found guilty of Implied Consent. And, if you refuse the breath test, assumption of guilt is automatic … even though that violates the concept of being innocent until proven guilty.

Following a municipal court trial, I found myself trying Tom's case in Circuit Court. My client was charged with his first DWI and with Implied Consent. The jury selection process—*voir dire*—eventually concluded, and John Bynum and I had picked the requisite dozen jurors. Of course, Mr. Bynum was trying to convince the jury that Tom was driving while intoxicated, and he presented a pretty strong case.

Then it was my turn. I had gone to the Detention Center and reviewed the tape. When arresting officers brought in suspects, the suspects had to sit and wait before they took the breath test. Because he had refused the test, Tom had a long wait.

I showed the videotape to the jury. The entire 25-minute video showed Tom sitting quietly on the bench, twiddling his thumbs. All the time, he appeared very polite and cooperative. The jury saw a polite young man sitting up, looking alert, talking without slurring, for the entire duration of the video. Even though it was very difficult to get a not-guilty verdict in a Pope County DWI case—Pope County has long been a dry county—I won the case.

Put simply, the jury did not think the prosecutor had met the burden of proof … particularly since there was no breath test. Luckily for Tom, the Implied Consent charge was overlooked and Tom's Driver's License was not suspended. He walked out of the courtroom unscathed.

I've already mentioned that I do not drink; similarly, I had never used illegal or illicit drugs. Consequently, misdemeanor drug cases always intrigued me. I found it interesting that possession of drug paraphernalia, which was a Class D felony at the time, carried up to six years in the penitentiary. This charge, however, would be reduced to simple misdemeanor involving what the law referred to as an "instrument of a crime." If my client was caught with an ounce or more of marijuana, he would be charged with a 'C' felony which carried a 3- to 10-year prison sentence and a fine. For whatever reason, "instrument of a crime" always made me think of guns and knives rather than a pipe used to smoke marijuana or crack cocaine.

I would negotiate the felony charge to a misdemeanor. Usually, my client would have no jail time, but the fines were always well above $500.

My client, Greg, was driving his flashy red Corvette down Interstate 40. Unbeknownst to Greg, his left taillight was out. When he hit his brakes to avoid a sock-eyed doe that flashed in front of him, an Arkansas State Trooper was directly behind him. Suddenly, flashing blue lights appeared in Greg's rearview mirror.

Greg pulled over and waited for the officer to tell him what he'd done wrong; he knew he wasn't speeding. With a State Trooper following you, why would you?

"Son," he said, "your left taillight is out." As the officer looked through the driver's window, he saw a suspicious looking pipe with a little residue on Greg's dash. Greg had been about to smoke the little bit of marijuana that remained in the pale green marble pipe.

The officer said, "Is that your pipe, Son?"

"Uh, yes." said Greg.

"Well, step out of the vehicle and let me pat you down for a weapon."

Greg suddenly remembered he had a pistol beneath the front passenger's seat. Greg panicked, because he was carrying the gun illegally and knew the State Trooper would find the weapon. Greg told me he was carrying the handgun in case his car broke down in an isolated area.

The State Trooper put Greg under arrest and took him to the Pope County Detention Center. Once there, Greg was charged with felony possession of drug paraphernalia, possession of marijuana, and the broken taillight. Amazingly enough, the Trooper ignored the firearms violation because he believed that every man had the right to defend himself. The Trooper actually testified to this point at Greg's bond hearing!

Greg was a student at Arkansas Tech University. Despite the flashy sports car, his financial means were quite limited. Consequently, I was appointed to represent him on the pair of felony charges and on the misdemeanor taillight charge as well.

I remember I was paid a maximum of $250 to work out a plea. Russellville's City Attorney, Don Bourne, who was also our deputy Prosecuting Attorney, informed me that felony possession of drug paraphernalia could be reduced to a misdemeanor. The two remaining misdemeanor charges only carried small fines, but the Instrument of a Crime carried hefty $600 fine. At least this three-misdemeanor plea agreement meant that Greg received credit for time served and could avoid serving additional time in jail. In fact, he spent but one night in jail before his parents bailed him out. Interestingly, Greg's parents were the reason Greg smoked marijuana in the first place; they'd been smoking marijuana *with* Greg from the time he was 13 years old.

My years of experience handling misdemeanor cases taught me an important lesson: The wheels of justice sometimes turn a little faster when you can work out a plea agreement in municipal court. I was always relieved to help my client avoid a felony conviction! Convicted felons cannot even vote. Even if the felony conviction is expunged at some point, convicted felons cannot own or possess a firearm, unless the Governor issues a pardon. Like many Arkansans, Greg liked guns and hunting deer, so escaping a felony conviction was rather a handy thing.

For a small fee, I represented men and women who were charged with petty misdemeanors. Interestingly, they would rather pay me over $400 in fees for a citation that would have incurred a total fine and costs of around $300.

I represented clients for running a red light, running a stop sign, driving left of the center line, and criminal mischief. "Criminal mischief" involved acts like graffiti or toilet-papering a house. Many times, these minor offenses were committed by minors ... someone under the age of 18. The Circuit Court had a 'juvenile court' division; the prosecuting attorney had to decide whether to send the case to juvenile court, where there would be no permanent criminal record, or leave it in adult court, where the juvenile risked having a criminal record for the rest of his life. I remember a juvenile who spray-painted his neighbor's car. Since he was young, his case went to juvenile court. If the case was a serious felony—a murder, robbery or rape, for example—the case usually remained in adult court.

When I was negotiating a plea for my client, a clean record on their part was decidedly helpful. If my client could pay the fine and costs upfront, I usually could keep the offense off their criminal record, which helped them when they were applying for jobs. If the violation was a moving violation, which meant it involved a moving vehicle, my client's auto insurance would never know about the infraction.

When Joe came to me for help, he was a truck driver and driving a big 18-wheeler. On the Interstate, where the speed limit was 70 for trucks, Joe was going 95. He tried to convince me that the officer's radar malfunctioned. Fines for truckers going 25 miles per hour or more over the speed limit were hefty, to say the least. Joe paid the fine for speeding; the ticket was on his driving record as well. Because Joe wanted a trial, I could not keep the conviction off his record.

My client Nick committed an interesting speeding violation. Like Joe, he drove an 18-wheeler for a living. On Interstate 40, passing through Russellville, Nick was going 15 miles per hour over the speed limit. Following the last time I'd represented a truck driver, Arkansas had decided to get tough on speeding truckers. The fine had increased to well over $1000.

Nick was incredulous because he'd only been speeding … not committing some sort of heinous crime. I called the deputy prosecutor, who was a friend. He usually worked out speeding tickets with me. After I told him the facts, he told me he wouldn't put up with truck drivers going 15 miles per hour over the speed limit! "They can kill someone going that speed," the man said.

"My poor client is just trying to make a living," I replied. By the end of the conversation, I had begged to the point that the deputy prosecutor allowed my client to keep the conviction off his record, but he did have to pay a fine that exceeded $1000.

In the United States, we are not supposed to have a debtor's prison. However, if you write a hot check for more than several hundred dollars, you are charged with a felony and put in jail. You do get a bond hearing, but if you cannot make bond, for whatever reason, you sit in jail. Therefore, the jail is like a debtor's prison. The way the statute is written, if you have insufficient funds in the bank when you write the check, or if you write a check on a closed bank account, you're in violation of the hot check law. Years ago, of course, many people were well-practiced in the art of kiting checks and trying to use money they didn't have, which usually worked until the check bounced.

Lucy came to see me after bonding out on a felony hot check violation, and I remember she was quite distraught. A sweet young lady with big blue eyes, blonde hair and a pretty face, Lucy wrote over $2,500 worth of hot checks, which is an obvious violation of the hot check law. Without my help, Lucy was going to prison for 3 to 10 years and would be required to pay a rather substantial fine in addition to the $2,500 she owed in restitution.

I charged Lucy a reasonable fee, then I went cap in hand to the prosecutor's office. After a little begging on my part, the prosecutor reduced the charge to a misdemeanor so Lucy did not have a felony record. The caveat was that Lucy had to pay full restitution immediately.

I begged Lucy's mother and father to pay the restitution so she would not be a convicted felon. In the end, her parents came through. The restitution was paid and Lucy pled guilty to a misdemeanor hot check charge. Instead of a hefty fine, she paid court costs of $60 or so.

Of course, Lucy was happy for another reason: Admitting on a job application that you are a convicted felon often precludes you from getting that job! Not many people get a second chance at anything, but Lucy did. I went home that evening hoping she appreciated her good fortune.

When I represented a client, whether for a hot check charge or something like a DWI, I usually got half my fee as a retainer. I allowed my clients to pay out the rest monthly. Sometimes, even though I'd won their case, they failed to pay me what they owed.

During my first year of law school, the professors drilled into our heads a singular thought: Never sue a client for unpaid attorney's fees. This action, at least in California, often allowed the client to sue you for malpractice. In that era, some attorneys were specializing in making cases against other attorneys.

I had my own personal solution to this Catch-22: I only sued for non-payment of fees when I had won my client's criminal case or custody fight. Usually, when I sued the client for attorney's fees, they failed to answer and I got a default judgment for unpaid attorney's fees, costs and additional fees incurred in the suit. Of course, these additions made the original debt a good deal larger.

I collected on my judgments by garnishing the wages of past clients. Another technique involved attaching their car with a Writ of Attachment. The Sheriff's office would pick up the car, and the auto would be sold at a courthouse auction. I received the *net* proceeds to pay the judgment. Out of the gross amount came any payments due on the car. Often, the amount owing on the car meant I didn't receive very much.

Debt collection is typically akin to squeezing blood from a turnip. When you sue someone for a debt and get a judgment, all you get is a piece of paper. You then have to collect on the judgment to get any money at all. Collecting on a judgment can be a nasty job.

One local attorney I knew got a Writ of Attachment when a client didn't pay. He then had the Deputy Sheriff collect his client's Christmas presents from beneath the tree. The Deputy took all the presents to the attorney ... including the gifts meant for the client's children. While this sounds like something from *How the Grinch Stole Christmas,* it actually happened in Russellville, Arkansas.

I never collected other people's judgments; I just tried to collect on my own. For example, a father would hire me to obtain custody of his son. I would get a pretty hefty retainer, which amounted to a downpayment of sorts, and then I allowed the client to pay out the remaining $5000 to $7000 that a typical custody fight costs. I would often go to the custody hearing without being fully paid, since my client had faithfully promised to continue to pay me. I would win custody for my client, then have to sue him for the money he still owed me.

A judgment is good for 10 years. If I don't collect within 10 years, I can renew it for another 10 years. When I retired, I had 10 judgments of several thousand dollars each on which I'd never collected a dime. I prayed about it, and decided not to hire someone to collect on the judgments. I just let it go. If those clients for whom I'd won cases could stiff me and still live with themselves, so be it. I remain firmly convinced of the existence of some kind of cosmic karma … what goes around does indeed come around again.

CHAPTER EIGHT

Happiness is a Warm Puppy

As Charles Schulz observed some years ago, happiness is a warm puppy. That old adage is still true today … even in a law office. You might think it incongruous, but I had several dogs in my office at varying times while I was practicing, including a secretary's Basset Hound. If my secretary left Buddy at home, he ate the sheetrock! The dog destroyed her laundry room walls; when she returned home one evening, Buddy appeared to have tunneled out. There wasn't much left.

Out of necessity, the woman moved Buddy into my office during the workday. There wasn't much he could damage; the office was pretty austere. However, since my secretary's desk was at the front of the reception area, Buddy tried his best to greet each visitor or client with all the enthusiasm customary for dogs of his breed and size. Buddy would often get so excited when he met new people that he would wet on the just-refinished hardwood floor! Of course, his accidents were easy enough to mop up. We found it hard to stay mad at Buddy for very long. His big, sad eyes told us that Buddy knew when he had failed us.

At an animal rescue shelter in Atkins, Arkansas, I found Khaki, who was easily the most joyful dog I have ever owned. I was volunteering at the shelter, and I noticed Khaki principally because she was so large. Khaki weighed about 70 pounds, and had the face of a yellow Labrador Retriever. She had warm, chocolate eyes that practically begged me to release her from the small pen she shared with a Terrier mix.

Khaki had a long, feathery tail—like a Collie's tail—and a soft, thick coat. Yellow Labs have shorter, rather oily fur, which enables them to jump headlong into icy water and retrieve the waterfowl their owners have shot from the skies.

I met Khaki on a hot and humid July afternoon. To say that she was an active dog is an understatement; the owner of the rescue asked me if I was sure I could handle such a rambunctious animal!

"Sure," I replied. "I've had two grown Labs on leashes … one in each hand." The Labs that Bob and I shared were male and female, and I distinctly remember that trying to get them into the vet's office was an experience akin to being pulled apart!

I got Khaki out of the too-small pen and she ran immediately to a nearby dog dish, gulping down dog food in double-quick time. I caught Khaki and put her on a leash; she was about eight months old and very thin. Typically, Labs grow to their full weight by about eight months. Khaki's time in the shelter hadn't been very conducive to putting on weight.

Khaki and I headed down the primrose path, so to speak. This dog wanted to run, and we headed down the road at full tilt. By the time we reached the end of that country lane, I was tired and sweating, but Khaki wasn't even breathing hard. At that time, I was in my early 50s and I could keep up with Khaki. By the time I reached 60, I was no longer able to survive that kind of workout.

Daylight was fading as I finally walked Khaki back to her pen. Her brown eyes reproached me as I pushed her back into the small enclosure. I remember driving away from the shelter thinking about Khaki and the other 90 or so dogs and assorted cats and horses kept penned up or chained to a doghouse. I had animals enough at home, and rescuing every dog I saw was impossible.

My aging Yellow Lab, Ruby, had died that Labor Day. Ruby was 13; she'd certainly had a good life. I returned to the Atkins shelter a couple of weeks later, determined to find a Black Lab or a Lab mix. I looked at the cute puppies but eventually walked away, convinced that someone would adopt each of the furry balls. Then I saw Khaki again. She'd spent the past couple of months in the same small pen, and she seemed to want me to take her away from the shelter.

Well, I did. I'd made the drive to Atkins in my little Toyota Prius. I wasn't sure I could get Khaki folded into the car's backseat, and she frankly didn't have much interest in getting in on her own. With some pushing and shoving, she finally complied. We made the drive back to our hardscrabble hillside north of Dover. Khaki saw the deep woods and noticed a squirrel running up a tree. She must have smelled the water in the branch of Mill Creek that runs through our property. Once released from the confines of the Prius, Khaki ran up and down the hillside. I've never seen such a joyful dog.

At about eleven months of age, Khaki had never been allowed to jump in a pond or creek. Of course, dogs can learn to swim while they're very young, but Khaki didn't know how. I remember leading her to a shallow part of Mill Creek; she sniffed the water and put her tongue into the cool stream. The water was good—just like the water in her bowl—and Khaki drank and drank. I gently put her front paws into the creek. I imagine the cool water running over her paws was a new sensation for the dog. She leapt into the water and I actually heard her belly hit the creek.

That winter, we had heavy snow. I made a snowball on the hillside; Khaki watched me. She knew what a ball was, and she knew how to play. I bent down and pushed the snowball down the hill, then watched as it grew bigger and bigger. Of course, Khaki couldn't resist, but I imagine she found it disconcerting to keep chasing a snowball that kept disappearing into the snow. Khaki would put her muff to the ground and shovel in snow as she walked. Watching her induced laughter.

Because I was fortunate enough to enjoy that sort of idyllic existence at home, I guess it's no wonder that I brought still more dogs into my office. A series of remarkable secretaries cherished the dogs as much as I did. Had they not liked dogs, these women wouldn't have lasted long in my practice!

Ashlee was the last secretary I hired, and also one of the best legal secretaries I ever had. She was not trained as a paralegal, and had only a high school diploma. Ashlee wanted to go to college, but she had married young and already had three children, so she had difficulty realizing that ambition.

Ashlee thought I was funny. I do admit to having a strange sense of humor. When I was about 60, I thought about trying to make stand-up comedy my vocation. Unfortunately, I was derelict; I finally retired the month after I turned 63. I drew Social Security forthwith, thinking that by the time I was in my 70s, there might be very little money left in the Social Security system.

Ashlee was the most conscientious worker I'd ever met. A male colleague, on the other hand, had perhaps the least conscientious—or honest—secretary on the planet. This young woman could barely type ('Typing' was the archaic term for 'keyboarding') and was a single mom with two children. Still, Caitlyn seemed sweet enough; she was a blonde with a nice figure.

My attorney friend kept several hundred dollars in cash in his desk drawer. At the end of each day, he kept finding himself about $200 short. After this shortfall had been repeated three or four times, he bought a surveillance camera. Only Caitlyn knew about the camera. Well, the camera disappeared ... along with more money! Caitlyn had stolen both the cash and the camera.

My friend sent Caitlyn on her way with the proverbial apple and a roadmap. If you're fired, you can only claim unemployment benefits if you haven't stolen from your employer or used physical violence in any way. Consequently, Caitlyn wasn't able to qualify for unemployment compensation.

Maybe my friend's experience with Caitlyn made me appreciate Ashlee for what she is: A remarkable young woman who loved her husband, her children, and animals of all kinds. Of course, Ashlee also loved dogs as much as I do. We both enjoyed Marco Polo, who was a black-and-white rat terrier with bushy brown eyebrows and a black-and-white body. In many respects, Marco Polo was my first house dog and first office dog as well.

Rat terriers hail from the United Kingdom. Bred to catch rats, they have always borne an appropriate breed designation. Marco Polo would snatch up a mouse and shake it in his jaws to kill it. He barked when he saw squirrels gobbling up seed from our bird feeders, and would probably have gone after them had the opportunity presented itself.

We got Marco Polo over in Dardanelle, a community on the Arkansas River about five miles south of Russellville. He was a tiny puppy; when he reached full size, he weighed only 19 pounds. Marco Polo was just too cute and too vulnerable to leave outside. His favorite trick was to jump on our bed and 'go undercover.' He'd worm his way beneath the blankets and sleep soundly all night. Sleeping with Marco Polo was like sleeping with a U-Boat commander.

When we went camping, Marco Polo crawled into my sleeping bag and slept at my feet. I was always afraid he'd suffocate, but the dog slept like a baby.

Even though he was not bred as a retriever, Marco Polo was obsessed by tennis balls. Bob and I would sit on the sofa; Marco Polo would bring the ball and place it in our upturned hands. This sort of subtle messaging worked well enough; we spent a lot of time throwing the tennis ball so the dog could fetch it back.

At my office, Marco Polo would sit at the back of my cushiony office chair and sleep the day away. My secretary would bring clients into my office; as long as I stayed seated, no one ever knew a dog was snoozing behind me.

Lenny, a Jack Russell and Rat Terrier mix, essentially grew up in my law office. Lenny is white with orangish brown markings … on his back, the dog has a brown spot in the shape of Mickey Mouse's head. We probably should have named Lenny 'Mickey' instead, but for some reason, Bob and I liked 'Lenny.' As a young dog, Lenny was like rubber; he would stretch out across our waterbed and extend to twice his usual length. Bob liked to call him 'Stretch.'

Ashlee loved having Lenny around the office as much as I did. We had a tug of war, from time to time, over who got to take care of Lenny and take him outside. I would emerge from my office to find Ashlee keyboarding with Lenny asleep on her lap.

Lenny went to work with me every day, but he spent the weekends roaming our hundred-acre woods. A warm and cuddly puppy makes any enterprise a joyful place to be. Many days, I found spending time with Lenny preferable to spending time with my clients … a sentiment other lawyers will likely appreciate.

Bob retired from Arkansas Tech at age 65. By the time Lenny was a year old, he had grown too rambunctious for office life. The little dog began staying at home with Bob. Bob loved throwing a tennis ball for Lenny to retrieve; I imagine Bob was enjoying the memories of Marco Polo doing the same thing. Even now, every visitor to our home will find Lenny barking for attention, and a tennis ball is sure to be hidden nearby. Suffice it to say that Lenny has become a bit obsessive about chasing a ball!

Dogs brought peace and kindness to my law office. I was always a better lawyer when I was keeping a dog in my office. My heart was filled with joy as I held my little Rat Terrier or Jack-Rat. To this day, I often prefer dogs to people.

The most unusual animal in my two-story office: A bat. A secretary and I were downstairs on a Tuesday afternoon. Suddenly, a bat came flying down the staircase. I opened the front door and it flew out into the bright sunshine. The bat had apparently been living in my attic.

I had other critters living there as well. Squirrels would chew holes in the soffit and birds would nest there. I could hear the squirrels scurrying about when I was upstairs. A wonderfully huge groundhog lived beneath an old chicken house in my back of my office property. We cohabitated peacefully for many years.

Today, I have three dogs and a very small flock of sheep. And no, I never took sheep to my office. They remained on my hundred-acre property in northern Pope County. The rather 'amateur' nature of our sheep operation was evident from the start, I suppose, when my husband acquired three rams—the father, Butthead, and two sons, Ringo and Starr. Butthead had broken his former owner's thigh. Without consulting me, Bob took in all three rams. I blame Bob's affinity for the Beatles! We had three very frustrated rams … we had no ewes. However, we soon remedied that situation.

A friend gave us an unusual ewe … unusual in the sense that the ewe had no wool. When we got her, she was about a year old. We named her 'Lambsie.' Kane rode in the back of the pickup truck with the ewe. We gave away Butthead and Starr, and kept Ringo with Lambsie. They had twin lambs. I don't think there's anything as cute as a newborn lamb. A lamb can stand up and walk at birth. The ewe licks off the lamb, and the lamb begins to nurse almost immediately.

When Lambsie was about 10 years old, she had twins again. She knew she lacked milk for both, so she kept knocking little Sweet Pea away. I watched this for about a day, then bought powdered milk and a bottle and fed the all-white lamb myself. I moved her into the basement of our house so I could bottle-feed her. Sweet Pea spent the nights in our bathroom with the door closed. During the day, she spent time on the decks around our house. A table with trash bags over it became a shelter against the rain, and Lambsie happily took refuge there. When I moved her into the basement, I had to repair and repaint the bathroom.

Our basement is a 1000-square-foot concrete slab with cement block walls. We live in a flood plain, and if the creek rises, we can open our doors and let the water flow through. I penned off part of the basement for Sweet Pea. In springtime, the basement is pleasant enough. I put newspapers down each day and changed them every night.

Taking care of Sweet Pea meant feeding her 3 or 4 times daily. I did try to reintroduce her to the flock. I had to carry her down our stairs, across our bridge and out to the meadow. If she got near her mama or the ram, they'd butt her away. After several attempts to reunite her with the flock, I gave up. Sweet Pea had outgrown my ability to carry her. We found her a good home with a family, but I cried as they drove off. I'd become quite attached to her. Since then, I've never taken a lamb into my home!

The most breathtaking scene I've ever seen—even with all the countries I've visited—was in my 4-acre sheep meadow. There was fresh snow on the ground, and my white ewe and her 3 pure white lambs stood in the pasture. For whatever reason, I felt very close to God at that point.

I also had lambs that were white with black spots. We called the ewe Dotty, and the spotted ram was Chocolate Chip, or 'CC' for short. After 22 years, I now have a black-and-white ram, Trés, and a spotted ewe, Whitey. Because I breed the sheep, I've had up to 16 at any one time. I buy them sweet feed and hay, which can get quite expensive. However, my sheep are worth the expense.

We had goats and sheep, which can be kept in the same pen. When a sheep and goat breed, it's called a *geep* or a *shoat.* Our neighbors had two goats, Oreo and Gump. Oreo was a black-and-white spotted goat, and Gump was white with a black head and neck. When they were born, their mother, a nanny goat, had no milk for them. Kane and I helped bottle-fed the cute kids for weeks.

Compared to sheep, goats are quite smart. Our two goats, in particular, were quite smart. They came up with a way to go through the doggy door into our house! The goats then jumped up onto the kitchen island and helped themselves to whatever food happened to be there. When we found them, they had also relieved themselves on the island. The sheer magnitude of the mess was unbelievable.

Gump was slower than the average goat; Oreo was the ringleader. We introduced them to our flock of sheep, and they assimilated well. When my ewes got pregnant, Oreo decided to try butting the ewes in the side. She didn't knock them over, but she was quite aggressive.

The goats were great escape artists, and they could come up with endless ways to get out of our pasture. The placid sheep, in contrast, stayed in the pasture. Oreo, the milk-less nanny goat, wound up bossing the sheep … including the ram! This was amazing to watch: A small nanny goat leading a big ram around.

We've had no goats since, for which our sheep continue to thank us.

CHAPTER NINE

Travel – My Remedy for Burnout

Burnout is a classic symptom for the overworked attorney. During my first two years in practice, I took no vacation time ... no time off for anything, for that matter. My only real breaks were the Monday holidays like Martin Luther King Day. I also closed when the courthouse closed for Thanksgiving, Christmas, New Year's Day and the Fourth of July.

After my first three years of practicing law—and even working weekends to finish my appellate briefs—I was suffering major burnout. My husband Bob and I went hiking on the Ozark Highlands Trail in the center of the Ozark National Forest. We backpacked for four days and three nights. We set up our camp beside a burbling creek. The rushing water lulled me to sleep ... literally, the stuff dreams are made of. I remember that I took a whole week off that year, and I needed the time away.

I found that traveling gave me a badly needed break from practicing law. I didn't have to argue at all on vacations. I found real relaxation in traveling the world and learning about other cultures. Of course, after taking a week or two off work, I had a good deal to catch up on. Some of my clients seemed very upset that I had taken time off. I learned the hard way that sometimes, rest and relaxation came at something of a cost to others.

The longest vacation Bob and I ever took was to Australia. We had to drive two hours just to get to the Little Rock airport. From there to Sydney, Australia, was a 26-hour trip. Our plane landed in Sydney, and we spent one night. The next day, we flew up to northern Australia. Bob and I snorkeled on the Great Barrier Reef. Sea cucumbers thrived in the shallow water, and the fish seemed to enjoy swimming with us. We also went into a wildlife refuge. The pelicans were five feet tall; at feeding time, they were quite demanding. We had to be really quick handing over their food. I don't know how we kept from getting our hands or fingers bitten off.

In the refuge, I walked inside the fence. There were two-foot-tall wallabies. They are beautiful, reddish marsupials. The wallabies stole my heart; the little wallaby I was feeding ate quite delicately from my hand. We fed them sweet potato squares. I thought the wallabies were much cuter than their kangaroo cousins.

We did stop in Melbourne, where they had the audacity to have wallaby on the menu. I told Bob we were *not* going into that restaurant, and we didn't. Bob didn't eat any wallaby, but he did eat kangaroo hors d'oeuvres.

Australia has the oldest tree, the oldest river, and the best of everything … according to the locals, anyway. Our guides were very proud of their continent, and they helped us sample local life. For example, an Australian barbecue has no sauce. The locals just cook meat on a grill. The kangaroo hors d'oeuvres excepted, we had a wonderful feast. My grilled steak was delicious, but I missed the sweet tang of American barbecue sauce.

My favorite Australian experience was holding a little koala bear named Cody. His little paw grabbed my right breast as I held onto his oily thick fur. I had thought koalas would be soft, but Cody had more oil on his fur than a Labrador Retriever. Holding a koala was something on my 'bucket list,' and Cody made that a unique experience indeed.

The Ghan is regarded as one of the world's great train journeys, and our trip certainly lived up to the billing. In all, we visited three different places in the Outback. We spent four days on the train; my favorite stop on The Ghan was in Coober Pedy, which is the opal capital of the world. Local legend held that if a person excavated there to create an underground house, they would find enough opals to almost pay for the house! However, most the homes are underground. All you can see from the road is a chimney with smoke coming out.

We got to take a tour of an underground house, which was an incredible experience. I almost wanted to move to Coober Pedy! However, I'm a southerner at heart, and Australia has quite cold winters, so I decided to stay in Arkansas.

Our next stop was Melbourne, where we got to see the smallest penguins in the world. At dusk, we sat right on the shore and the penguins came wading in, waddling toward us in a triangle formation. They came right up to us and we were close enough to touch them. Unfortunately, you weren't allowed to touch or even take photos of the little critters because a camera flash will blind them.

Then we flew on to Sydney, the capitol of Australia. In the tallest building in Australia, I took an elevator to the top and saw a great view of the harbor. The only part of Australia we didn't traverse was the western part of the country, where Perth is located. We simply ran out of time, which is an odd thing to say about a 21-day trip. Going to Australia was the most amazing and incredible vacation I ever took … I felt as if I were in a movie the entire time. But when we got back to the United States after three weeks, I was glad to be back home.

Both Bob and our son, Kane, loved riding on trains. In 2006, we took a Canadian passenger train that went from Halifax, Nova Scotia to Montreal, Quebec. To get to Halifax, we had to fly in on a dark, gloomy, rainy night. We had travelled without umbrellas, and we were drenched. Nova Scotia was like being in a miniature part of the United Kingdom. The towns there reminded me strongly of England, Scotland and Ireland.

Next, we visited St Edward's Island, a small province where the book, *Anne of Green Gables,* originated. I'd read Lucy Maud

Montgomery's book when I was a girl, and I'd always wanted to see that part of the country. Then we were off on a passenger train headed to Montreal. The train had sleeper cars with bunk beds and a bathroom. Kane had his own private room next to ours. He was 16, and for the first time, I saw him flirt with girls. We had no way to know that Kane's time had nearly run out.

That trip itself was little short of amazing. The train's observation deck was made of glass. The deck was the top of a two-deck car. There I would sit for hours, viewing the beautiful landscape. We met a very nice couple from South Africa and became friends.

Montreal was surreal, because you heard people speaking French rather than speaking English. Our son was able to use his two years of French classes to good advantage; Kane spoke to the locals and told us what the signs said. He genuinely enjoyed being our tour guide. I'd taken French nearly 35 years before and had forgotten much of what I'd learned.

Bob and Kane explored Montreal while I attended the International Kiwanis Convention. At the Convention, I was fascinated by the procession of Kiwanians carrying the flags of all the countries that had Kiwanis clubs. The long banner procession gave me chills, and I remember the feeling of pride because I was a Kiwanian.

After Kane was killed in a car accident in February, 2007, Bob and I needed to get away—far away. We planned a trip to northern Europe and flew into Brussels, Belgium. Because Brussels was the first European city I ever saw, it will probably always be my favorite. The streets are cobblestone, and we stayed in the historic district rather than opting for the more modern commercial section of Brussels. Our old hotel was in a beautiful square, surrounded by other old buildings. When you looked up, the second, third and fourth stories all had marble statutes of people beside the windows.

In northern Europe, the policemen do not carry guns. I felt peaceful in that relaxed atmosphere. Bob's favorite part of Brussels was the statute of the little boy peeing, which is a water fountain and a popular tourist attraction. The statue is dressed in different costumes depending on the season or time of the year. I took several pictures of Bob standing beside the peeing boy.

In Belgium, I ate the best chocolate caramels I've ever had. After more than 17 years of traveling the world, I have never found caramels as good as those in Brussels. Belgian chocolate has much to recommend it!

Just as we had in Australia, we traversed northern Europe by train. Our next stop was Amsterdam, in the Netherlands. Amsterdam is a beautiful city. The hydrangeas really 'popped' because they were blue, pink, purple and white. Hydrangea bushes lined the river. Bob and I decided to take a boat ride. As it happened, our guide did not want to go back to work, so he took us on a 2 1/2 hour ride down the canals of the city. We wound up sailing in the ocean outside of Amsterdam.

We also visited Amsterdam's red-light district. We saw the women lying out, sunning, getting ready for the night's work. We marveled at the sheer number of bicycles, only exceeded by Chinese cities like Beijing.

Our next destination was Copenhagen, Denmark. We toured the Kronborg castle, where Shakespeare set *Hamlet.* Kronborg is one of the most important castles in northern Europe, and it is easily the most beautiful castle I have ever seen. I grew up loving fairy tales, which typically involved castles. Of course, I was the beautiful princess waiting to be rescued by a handsome prince. That kind of situation is all too easy to imagine in a setting like Kronborg.

Copenhagen's claim to fame is a culinary treat that reflects the country of origin: The Danish. When you take a bite of a *real* Danish danish, the pastry absolutely melts in your mouth, and the taste of sweet icing lingers like a scented kiss.

From Copenhagen, we took a boat across to Sweden. In Sweden, we toured the castle that faces the Kronborg castle. Over the centuries, these two castles have actually fired cannons at each other! We stayed for lunch and then toured the town. Bob and I felt Kane's absence quite keenly, but we managed to enjoy most of the trip.

We took the train ferry to Germany. The entire train was loaded onto a ferry and we sailed aboard. We wound up in Berlin; Bob wanted to see the historical parts of the city that remain after the intensive Allied bombing that ended World War II. We toured the Holocaust Memorial and museum, which was incredibly sad. The Berlin Wall had come down in 1989, and we walked the remnants of the wall which had divided east and west Germany.

I toured the Berlin aquarium by myself and enjoyed the coral reef fish and whales. Bob toured the World War II sites, which I had no real interest in seeing. The best hotel of the trip was in Berlin. I remember that the hotel had a wonderful free breakfast buffet where I stuffed myself every morning.

After touring five countries in two weeks, I kissed the ground when I returned to the United States. Bob and I were happy to be back home, but we knew we would go back to Europe, and we did.

A couple of years later, Bob and I flew into London and rode a hop-on, hop-off bus to see the city's splendid sights. Viewing London from a sightseeing bus helps you narrow down the places where you want to spend time. The old city is too vast to try to see more than a place or two per day. Bob and I loved the double-decker buses, and we rode them at every opportunity.

Our boat ride down the Thames took us beneath Tower Bridge. We stood outside Buckingham Palace, and I particularly enjoyed the gorgeous statues that abound in the West End. We were in London over July 4, and it seemed unusual not to have fireworks and celebrations. Another thing we found wanting was rain! There simply was none. In fact, London was setting heat records … and our hotel room had no air conditioning. We did the best we could to cope with the heat, which was affecting the locals as well.

Next, we headed to Scotland. I think we got rain one day, but at least Scotland was cooler and somewhat windy. We went to Loch Ness, where Bob took the usual tourist boat ride in a vain effort to locate the Loch Ness monster. Every local gift shop was filled with replicas, small and big, of 'Nessie.' Since I am not a believer, I felt like a wretched outcast.

In Wales, we visited a castle built in 1066. This was a museum recreation done to a high standard; period furniture made it look as if someone actually lived there. We stayed in a little bed and breakfast that was owned by a couple who had moved to Wales to escape the sectarian violence in Northern Ireland. Like our hosts, the Welsh townspeople were decidedly more friendly than folks in London had been, and I grew to like the country very much.

I had never thought a trip to Iceland would be particularly interesting, but ours was. We flew into Reykjavik and spent two days there. We saw throngs of puffins on the shoreline. I even bought a puffin shirt! Our tour was planned via a GPS—pretty novel technology in Iceland at that time—that took us to new and different places each day. Bob navigated while I drove around Iceland back to Reykjavik. We both enjoyed the spectacular waterfalls ... especially the Gullfoss, which is native parlance for 'golden falls.' We even saw volcanoes.

In the lakes, there was glacier ice the color of blue Kool-aid. What appears to be greenish grass in Iceland is actually green moss on the rocks, boulders and plains. Moss takes years to grow in the local climate, and we were careful not to disturb it.

The one national forest in Iceland would more properly be called a 'woods' in northwest Arkansas. There are actually very few trees in Iceland, and much of the timber that was there was cut down to build houses. The natives import trees so the forests will grow more rapidly. We spent a day in the woods and enjoyed the brief respite from our homesickness.

If there are few native trees in Iceland, there are even fewer fences. As a consequence, sheep tend to roam wide and free, feeding on the grass on the side slopes of the roadways. Driving there tended to be a bit nerve-wracking; I nearly hit a couple of sheep.

Another trip took us to Anchorage, Alaska, where we rented an RV and drove more than 1500 miles through some very unsettled country. Bob and I enjoyed Mount Denali State Park, and I remember we got there on a beautiful, sunny morning. There were grizzly bear, bighorn sheep and antelope. Hawks flew overhead. We watched in amazement as a bear tried to kill a baby elk. The elk was in a pond with its mother and somehow managed to survive the bear's onslaught.

Grizzly bears are an interesting species. When a grizzly has a cub, she nurses her young and doesn't go into heat again for some time. Male grizzly bears will try to kill the babies so the mother's favors become more immediately available. The frazzled logic here was readily apparent; few other species try to kill their young so they can have more babies! We did see a grizzly chasing a baby bear, but the baby managed to escape unscathed.

Along the roadway, we spotted a mother moose and her baby lolling in a pond. This was the first moose I'd ever seen in the wild. We settled into our campground as salmon were spawning. I watched in wonder as salmon headed back upstream to their breeding ground. I also discovered that fresh salmon is quite a delicacy compared to the canned stuff one buys in the grocery store.

On a one-day boat cruise, we saw dozens of sea lions. They feed on the puffins on nearby rocks. We floated past glaciers that were calving, which means that part of the glacier would fall off and crash into the water below. Once again, the glacier ice had that interesting intense blue hue—something akin to blue Kool-aid. We even spotted a humpback whale en route to summertime feeding grounds.

In mid-summer, Alaska doesn't get dark until very early in the morning, then the dawn comes a couple of hours later. We had to close the RV blinds so we could get some sleep. Even though we were in a part of the United States on July 4, there were no fireworks … the sky never got dark enough.

In many ways, Alaska is the final frontier. In 2022, Jim and I took a cruise to Juneau, Sitka and Skagway. En route back to Seattle, the ship stopped in Victoria, British Columbia. The ocean was beautiful, and we enjoyed the cruise even though the ship was crowded and the weather was somewhat unpredictable. A couple of our day excursions were nearly rained out! I remember walking through the streets of Juneau with Jim and wandering through the deserted state capitol. Jim wondered aloud what my father would have made of the fact that we were standing alone in the legislative chamber. I like to imagine Dad would have been impressed.

Just before Bob discovered he had cancer, we decided to visit Spain and Switzerland. We flew into Basil, which sits near the border with France, Germany, Italy and Austria. Perhaps that's why Switzerland has such wonderful Italian, French and German food. Growing up, I wanted to go to Switzerland and have their wonderful chocolate. I thought the glaciers and the Swiss Alps were magnificent.

Of course, I had to tour several castles in Switzerland, one of which was the Thun. Thun Castle was built in the 12th century, and houses the Thun Castle museum, which is a Swiss heritage site. We drove through Switzerland and saw beautiful glaciers and breathtaking views of the snowcapped Alps. The mountains looked down on crystal clear lakes.

To get to Mount Zermatt, we took a train. No cars are allowed in the quaint little town. Mount Zermatt was snow-covered and quite majestic. Naturally, the chocolate was to die for. As you might have deduced, I'm quite a chocoholic! When you eat chocolate, the chocolate actually releases Serotonin. Sitting with Bob, eating chocolate, I remember feeling decidedly euphoric.

I still plan to get to Morocco and Japan before I'm too old to travel. by that point, I will have been to six continents. I grew up with so many friends who have never left home. In comparison, I feel like quite the world traveller!

Sometimes, though, the best travel destinations are close by. When Kane was just 10 years old, we flew to Chicago. We stayed in a suburb and rode the train into downtown Chicago each day. That was the year of the *Cows on Parade* exhibition, and everywhere you looked, you saw beautifully painted statues of cows that were as tall as my boy. Even at that young age, Kane was quite tall.

We went to the Navy pier and toured some ships. I remember we also enjoyed an amusement park. The best art museum I've visited in the United States is the Art Institute of Chicago. The Institute has a wonderful collection of impressionist paintings. *Sunday Afternoon on the Island of LaGrande Jatte* by Georges Seurat is one of my favorite works, and it was one of the founding paintings of the neoimpressionist movement. When I finally saw it in person, I felt as if I were greeting an old friend for the very first time.

In downtown Chicago, Kane put on skates and cruised up and down the sidewalks. On that trip, we walked into the first Disney store we'd ever seen. Kane loved *101 Dalmatians* and *The Lion King*. He was enthralled by the plethora of stuffed toys and Disney t-shirts. The Chicago trip was a wonderful vacation, and it stands out in my memory today because I had the opportunity to expose our young son to so much art and culture.

I chose to raise my son in Arkansas because it is a beautiful state and quite bucolic. Unfortunately, Arkansas is also something of a cultural desert. The Waltons—of Walmart fame—did build Crystal Hills Art Museum in Rogers, Arkansas. The museum is a beautiful building, designed by a wonderful architect. However, the museum collection is only United States art. To get my impressionist 'fix,' I typically have to travel.

Travel opened my mind to art and new cultures. Today, travel to other countries is still one of my favorite activities.

CHAPTER TEN

Wills, Probate and Guardianships

For me, wills and probate were one of the most interesting areas of the law. Today, many people call the issues that revolve around wills and probate *estate planning.* Back when I started my office, the approach was a little less sophisticated. Clients would come in and summarize all the assets they owned, and then I would ask questions about their marital status, how many children they had, and other salient facts. All this was necessary before I could even draft a simple will. An uncontested will—one with no associated angst—cost around $100 for many years, which sounds ridiculously cheap. After I'd been in practice for some time, I raised the price to $250 for husband and wife wills. These were typically 'mirror wills' in which the couple essentially left everything to each other.

I also prepared trusts to avoid probate. Wills *must* be probated, whereas a revocable living trust helped *avoid* probate. A revocable living trust is preferable to a will because a will must be probated within 5 years of the decedent's death. This means hiring an attorney, filing a probate case, and serving notice on all heirs of the probate of the will. All this can cost a lot; attorney's fees depend on the value of the estate. For example, an estate worth $2,000,000 or $3,000,000 would cost much more to probate than an estate worth $200,000 or so.

The executor of the will usually must prepare an inventory listing all real and personal property. The value of each listed item must be included as well. The inventory becomes a part of the case file, and becomes a part of the public record. The record is available at the county courthouse, and anyone can view the assets … land, cars, jewelry, etc.

Many folks don't want all this to become public knowledge. If you have a revocable living trust, on the other hand, and all property is transferred into the trust, the heirs can avoid probate altogether.

When I prepared revocable living trusts for my clients, I would make sure all the assets were put into the trust. I would deed the land into the trust, along with all rolling stock—vehicles—and personal property. When someone had a CPA prepare a trust, the real and personal property often wouldn't be transferred into the trust. Any property not transferred would need to be probated, despite the lack of a will.

Creating a revocable living trust was a relatively private way to settle an estate, and one that saved a good deal of money in both costs and attorney's fees. Filing a will and providing notice of probate typically costs $300 to $400.

Notices of probate must be published in the local newspaper, and claimants must be given six months to file their claims. If my client had accumulated significant assets, like expensive cars and real estate, I always suggested that we prepare a revocable living trust rather than a simple will.

Esther hired me to prepare her will. She had four sons and two grandsons. One of her sons had stolen from her, so she disowned him and left him nothing. Some lawyers give the disowned person one dollar or $100; I always left them nothing because if they inherited even a dollar, they were a legal heir, and could effectively prevent the wheels of justice from turning smoothly.

Well, Esther died and we had quite a mess on our hands. Two of her three boys did inherit, but she had disinherited a son. Instead, she gave his share to his son, a grandson that she had helped raise. When Esther's will was read, the disinherited son chose not to hire a lawyer to contest. His son, Esther's grandson, got his own lawyer, but the other attorney wasn't really needed.

The problem was that Esther's estate was land-rich and cash poor. Consequently, the boys had angst over who would sell her land. Esther had owned about 100 acres, including some scenic hills and bluffs situated along a creek. The land had been in the family for generations. After a couple of years, the sons divided the land into parcels, with each getting an equal share. The case finally settled. There were several vehicles and a good quantity of antiques to divide up, but we finally wrapped up Esther's estate.

The next estate I was hired to probate was not so easy. The testator had five children. My client, Goldie, was appointed executor over the estate. She was one of the five children.

Unfortunately, Goldie did not talk to her brothers and sisters; nor did they speak to her. One asset caused a problem: A huge set of old phonograph records. In my opinion, the records were old and scratched. I don't know how anyone can fix scratched records; the vinyl tends to skip when you play it. Eventually, all the personal property was forced sold at an estate sale. I finally put that estate to rest, but it was a long haul.

Incidentally, heirs usually lose money when personal property goes to auction. People come to auctions for one reason: To get stuff cheap.

I was always amazed that people don't write their own will or hire an attorney to prepare a will for them. I particularly remember the estate of a widower who had no children. He was too cheap—or too lazy—to prepare a will. I saw a rather exotic draft of a convoluted will in which he was going to leave his substantial estate to various charities, one being his church. However, for lack of interest, he never executed the will. In other words, he never paid for it.

The man's parsimonious nature resulted in his estate being administered by the court rather than probated. An administrator is placed in charge of the estate if there is no will. Rose was the administrator of the court. Rose went over every day and fed the dead man's 15-year-old cat. After a year, Rose finally found it a new owner. Rose, it developed, had dogs at her house and they would not tolerate a cat in her home.

Most of this man's heirs were older, and they did not seem particularly desperate for money. In any event, the dead man had been dead for four years and the case was still unfinished. At issue were several parcels of land that effectively stalled completion of the case. The heirs fought about what to do with the land; some wanted to sell the real property, and others wanted to divide it in kind. Finally, the heirs hired an attorney. Since I was representing the administrator, Rose, I was glad the man's heirs had taken this step. I stepped out of the picture and let the new attorney wrap up the case.

When my father died in July, 2015, he left a will. As it happened, I was the attorney who probated his estate in court. I filed the will and we had a hearing to distribute his real and personal property. The original probate of my father's will was finalized with an Order of Distribution. However, my father owned a lot in Kosciusko County, Indiana, near the county seat of Warsaw. The singular distinguishing feature of lot was several beautiful walnut trees. When my father was in his 80s, he decided to deed the land to my sister and me. The problem: My father didn't like to spend money, so he broke the rule and wound up trying to do it all himself. As you may have heard, people who represent themselves typically have a fool for an attorney.

Anyway, Dad placed the land in my sister's name and my name, but in tandem with his own name. That made us all *tenants in common*. When my father died, his share of the Indiana property went to his estate. In his will, he left the property to my sister and me, but left 20 percent of his estate to a few of his favorite charities. The remaining 80 percent of the estate was divided between my sister and me.

To visualize what's happening here, imagine a piece of land is in a box. The box is the State of Indiana, and the land cannot be moved out of the box. Effectively, it is stuck in the box … stuck in Indiana. Since I'd already probated the will in Arkansas, what is required is an *ancillary* administration of the estate in Indiana. This means I would wind up probating the will in a state where my father had real property but did not reside there at the time of his death. Since Dad lived in Arkansas, the lot—which was worth about $5000—had to be probated separately in Indiana. The sticky wicket: Hiring an Indiana attorney to do the probate would cost about as much as the land was worth. After paying the commission to the realtor when we sold the land, my sister and I might even wind up in the hole!

To date, Dad's lot with the beautiful walnut trees sits empty. The good thing: The trees keep growing and won't be cut down anytime soon. Dad bought the land in the 1940s with the expectation that he and my mother would build a home there. However, dad wound up living most of his life in Arkansas. I hope the wildlife is enjoying the lot! No doubt, the squirrels are loving the walnuts.

If my dad was a unique individual, so were my clients. I saw a fair share of hoarders when I was probating an estate. A mild-mannered woman came to hire me about her mother's estate. I sat and listened patiently as she cried about her 80-year-old mother's tragic death. The older woman had lived quite a meaningful life; she had raised two daughters. Unfortunately, one daughter did not get along with the other. The remaining problem was the state of the estate house and how we would get rid of all the junk that was crammed into a few small rooms.

Actually, 'crammed' was an understatement; when I walked into the house, I could not even enter two of the rooms. Karen, my client, slept on the sofa after having uncluttered it for her long winter's nap. We ended up paying Karen's sister for her share and decluttering the house. Karen did not go away happily, but we finally got her mother's estate sorted.

A common misconception is that if you don't have a will, the state will take the estate and leave nothing to the legal heirs. I kept trying to tell people that this just wasn't true; if you don't leave a will, the assets will go to the closest heirs and be divided among them accordingly. If a person is married, the surviving spouse and any children will share the estate. If you die single and have no children, the property goes to your mother and father if they survive you. If your parents are already dead, your estate goes to your siblings. If a sibling has pre-deceased you, your estate goes to their children, who were your nephews and nieces.

I did a lot of estate planning doing wills and trusts. I enjoyed probating wills and settling the estate. People would ask me what area of law I enjoyed practicing the most. I would habitually reply, "I like variety. Whether I enjoy the case really depends on the client." Nowhere was this response more accurate than in the area of wills and probate! All 50 states have uniform wills and estates except for Louisiana, which is based on the Napoleonic code. I shied away from everything coming from Louisiana, because that state has such disparate laws and statutes compared to Arkansas and other moderate states.

I found that guardianships were an effective way to keep children out of the foster care system. At times, a mother or father becomes dependent on alcohol, illegal drugs, or both. A substance abuse problem could cause the parent to neglect or abuse their children. I saw alcohol destroy more marriages than methamphetamines.

In one case, the parents were high most of the time, and failed to feed their children or even buy food for them. The children did not get adequate sleep and were ill-clothed. Environmental neglect was the main cause of children being taken from their parents. They would go to foster care until the parents could get them returned to their home.

In the good cases, an aunt or grandparent would pass the home study and get custody of the minor children. I developed an ingenious plan; it would start with the grandparents consulting with me and describing the abuse and neglect their grandchildren were enduring. Next, I would be retained to file for an emergency guardianship. The judge would sign an *Ex Parte* Temporary Order of Custody.

Ex parte means there's no hearing or input from the other side. There had to be a hearing within a week or so so that the custodial parent could disprove the allegations of abuse or neglect. Usually, after the temporary hearing, the children would stay with the grandparent, aunt or uncle who had gotten temporary custody. I had accomplished keeping the children of tender years out of the less-than-acceptable foster care system.

In another case, a brother and sister were sent to an orphanage a couple hundred miles away from their home. Fortunately, I got them home within a couple of months, reunited with their mother and father.

There are guardianships over the person and over the estate. A guardianship over a person means the guardian takes care of the life choices. Such choices include where to go to school, whether the ward can marry, and other everyday decisions that a parent would make. Guardianship over the estate, on the other hand, is control over all money and property owned by the ward. If the ward is on SSI or Social Security, the guardian would control how that money was spent.

The same applies if a ward receives child support or any other income.

There are two types of guardianships based on age. One is for minors under 18 years of age, and the other is for adults. If a person is elderly or disabled and can no longer make life decisions or spend their money wisely, I would then file an Emergency Petition of Guardianship. Even though the person was an adult, the guardian would still make all the decisions for the ward, including medical and dental care, living accommodations and so on.

If a guardianship is in effect and the ward dies, the case is transferred into an estate, either probate of the will or administration of the estate. This was an easy way to begin an estate when someone passed away. My most common guardianship was when a person with special needs turned 18 years of age. As long as the person was under 18, the parent had custody. The day the ward turned 18, however, the custodial parent or parents lost all rights to make life decisions for the ward.

For the ward, it was very important to have a guardian. Otherwise, some nefarious individual could trick the ward and take their money or assets. A guardianship over the person was a way to protect a vulnerable individual from harm.

At my office, Kathy brought in her son, Clay, who was on Social Security because he had Down's Syndrome. Clay was turning 18 in a couple of months. Kathy was concerned that Clay would make unwise decisions, even though he was still in high school and living at home. I talked with Clay and asked him if it was okay if his mom was in charge of his money and would keep taking care of him. I got a resounding 'Yes!' Clay was blonde with sparkling green eyes; he hugged me when we were finished and I knew I had made a friend.

We drew up the papers for the Order of Guardianship. Clay had to sign a consent, which he did willingly.

Guardianships over an elderly person were far more convoluted. The spouse, son or daughter filed the petition, and the ward often felt they were competent to look after their own affairs. A spunky 80-year-old woman, Mildred, wasn't excited about her daughter having control of her and her money. I represented the guardian, not the ward. I had to obtain a doctor's letter stating that the person could no longer care for themselves independently and needed a person to be in control the real and personal property.

Mildred took umbrage with the letter. At the hearing, she told the judge that she was perfectly capable of taking care of herself and her money. The judge had to ascertain whether there was enough proof to set a guardianship in place. After a lengthy hearing, the judge appointed Mildred's daughter temporary guardian. Mildred could get an attorney and fight the guardianship at the final hearing. As it turned out, Mildred and her daughter made amends and we did not have to endure a final contested hearing.

Mildred's daughter, like all appointed guardians, had to file a yearly accounting with the court. She also had to file a yearly report stating whether Mildred had improved or gotten worse. If the disability resolved itself, the guardianship could be dismissed.

I genuinely enjoyed handling step-parent adoptions. Several times, I represented a parent with up to four children. The parent came to see me because the biological mom or dad had deserted them. The absent parent left the wife and children, seldom visited, and refused to pay court-ordered child support.

Failure to pay support and failure to visit your child for more than a year are both grounds to terminate the rights of non-custodial parents.

I remember one woman who brought her new husband to my office. She told me that her husband wanted to adopt her four boys. Since the father of the children had abandoned them, the father's rights were terminated and the adoption went through.

I always assured my client that I could get the judge to approve the adoption. But I always warned the client of a double-edged sword: If the parties separated, the other spouse could gain custody of the children. Legal parent status also conferred all parental rights, including custody of the children. The biological parent always had a big decision to make, since many seemingly good marriages end in divorce.

Sometimes, a client would decide against the step-parent adoption. Of course, giving the spouse equal rights to the client's children was always something of a risk.

I remember one client who told me she was going ahead with the step-parent adoption simply because her husband was the only father the children knew. In many cases like hers, the absent father was in prison. I felt I was truly helping when I handled step-parent adoption cases, because I gave the children a chance for real stability in their lives.

In one such adoption, the mother had three girls, ages 2 to 10. The stepdad was already supporting the three children. Since the biological dad wasn't visiting or supporting his children, the adoption went through speedily enough. All three children had their last names changed to the new father's last name.

I also handled regular adoptions, where the parents' rights were terminated, or where the parents consented to allow a childless couple to adopt a child. Most attorneys who handled adoptions had a connection with a doctor who had pregnant patients willing to give their babies up for adoption. The doctor would facilitate a meeting between the attorney and the expectant mother. At no cost to her, the lawyer would find a deserving, childless couple who could adopt her baby. The expectant mother would sign a Consent for Adoption before she gave birth. The mother would then have 10 days following the birth to change her mind and keep the newborn.

I never got a baby for adoption through a doctor. However, I did have a pregnant client, Sophie, who was going to prison for burglary and theft. She wanted to give up her baby boy. I found a childless couple who were dying to have a newborn boy! He was a beautiful baby; blonde hair, brown eyes and Gerber baby looks. Since Sophie had no idea who the biological father might have been, I had to come up with a way to gain consent from the biological father. The attorney who handled the adoption got the consent from a man who claimed to be the father, and the adoption went through.

In this day and age, of course, babies are sold on the black market. A California couple wanting to adopt would pay up to $100,000 so the biological parents would give their consent to the adoption. This was patently illegal, and I never had it occur in one of my adoption cases. Because I was an honest lawyer, I never got a portion of the 'finder's fee' that other attorneys received.

I also managed international adoptions. Margaret and her husband, Ben, adopted a baby from South Korea. The transaction was fascinating. The birth certificate and other documents were in Korean.

Surrogate mothers are another interesting aspect of adoptions. Silvia loved being pregnant, but she was already married with three children at home. She and her husband agreed that Silvia would be artificially inseminated with the sperm of the adoptive dad. Silvia got pregnant, and I represented the couple as they gave up their rights to the newborn. Silvia had two more babies for childless couples. I could never understand how she could give away her newborn, but she was paid $25,000 to $30,000 for being a surrogate.

By the end of my law career, even a single woman or a single man could adopt a child. I never handled a single-parent adoption. I never felt better about practicing law than I did when I found a baby for a childless couple who wanted to adopt.

Another type of hearing in probate was a commitment hearing. "I am God," my client exclaimed to me. After talking to Joe for about 20 minutes, he almost had me convinced that he *was* God!

The judge had asked me to represent Joe in his commitment hearing. The issue at the hearing was whether Joe was a danger to himself or others. The experts testified that Joe was hallucinating; however, Joe was convinced that he could forcibly take out the judge and anyone else who forced him to go to the State mental facility.

I did my best to calm Joe down. I patiently explained to Joe that he would just go stay in a nice hospital to get checked out. Since Joe was homeless, the idea of a bed and good food didn't seem too bad. I convinced him to go, and told him that the State hospital was always so busy that he wouldn't be there long. Usually, the State hospital had a revolving door … the patient was only there a day or two before they were discharged back to the cold, cruel world from whence they had come.

Another client I represented believed he was Jesus Christ. We had a long hearing in which he tried—unsuccessfully—to convince the judge of his true identity. He was committed to the State hospital.

Commitment hearings were a challenge, but I tried to represent my client as well as I could. For some, my efforts would never be good enough.

I enjoyed handling adoptions and guardianships. I felt a certain satisfaction keeping children out of the broken foster care system. I enjoyed helping disabled and elderly individuals have a sound guardian to look over their estate. I truly felt I had served others when I finished a guardianship or a happy adoption for a childless couple. These two things were probably my favorite areas of practice, and those areas of the law gave me the greatest satisfaction.

CHAPTER ELEVEN

Places in the Heart

EARLY ON, I CONCLUDED THAT law offices tend to reflect the personality of the lawyers who own or run them. Some law offices are pretty bare-bones, because underneath their nice suits, lawyers, like doctors, are simple tradespeople. In comparison, other law offices look quite opulent. From the start, I wanted my office to reflect my no-nonsense approach to serving my clients. By the time my son died, in 2007, my law office had become a second home … a refuge of sorts that I both needed and appreciated.

My very first office was on South Boulder Street in Russellville. I rented it from another local attorney, Dale Braden. I remember there was a compass on the linoleum reception room floor. I could only afford a secretary for three hours a day, and a secretary was a necessity so people would not think I was the secretary!

Attorney Dennis Sutterfield had an office down the street, and his mother was his secretary. What a deal! My mother was never my secretary, but she did help me decorate my new office. Mama and I went around to used furniture stores and bought chairs, a loveseat and other furnishings. Then my father gave me his mahogany desk, which was large and impressive. At least I looked like a 'real' lawyer.

Back then, that was about the extent of the positive side of my balance sheet. When I started, I had no money and no clients. All attorneys are not rich … certainly, not at first. My little practice took about six months to show a profit.

My next door neighbor was John Bynum, another local attorney. We shared a bathroom and a back hallway. Because I had no income to speak of, I soon became aware of the fact *I* was the one paying for the toilet paper and paper towels for the bathroom. I thought this a ridiculous situation. To get John to pay his share, I took him a bill for a dollar. He chuckled, then handed me a dollar bill. From that point, John had his secretary, Kim, stock the bathroom.

After two years in that South Boulder Street office, I became partners with John Shermer and moved to South Commerce Street. I had my own office in his building. When the arrangement with John had run its course, I became partners with David Gibbons. Our office was on West Main, behind a men's clothing store.

Before we entered into our partnership, I told David that I was trying to get pregnant. I was 32, and my biological clock was ticking away.

"No problem," David said.

When I had Kane a year later, I was determined to breastfeed, and did so for the first year. Every day, during the noon hour, I had to pump breastmilk so Kane would have milk at daycare. Suddenly, the fact that I was a mother began causing problems in our law office. One day, David told me he thought I wasn't working hard enough.

David asked rather pointedly why Bob couldn't be up with Kane at night. Of course, since Bob wasn't nursing, Kane only wanted me. David apparently couldn't grasp this elemental aspect of parenting a newborn, but Bob and I certainly did.

When Kane was six months old, he came down with chicken pox. In fact, my son was the first baby in the daycare to contract the disease. I could only work half days, because Bob had to teach an early morning class. At that point, Kane wasn't sleeping well at night; he was very prone to ear infections and I was up with him every hour or two.

By June, 1990, Kane was nine months old. David essentially told me that I needed to leave the practice. When I moved out, I moved to One Main Place, which stood at the intersection of Highway 7 and Highway 64, Russellville's Main Street. Since I already had a husband, it occurred to me that I didn't need *another* man telling me what to do or how to do it. Actually, Bob never told me what to do, since he had no clue about how to run a business. The extent of Bob's sage advice: If I was too busy, I should charge more!

I was happy to be out on my own. I had no partner to constantly criticize me, which was quite liberating. At One Main Place, I literally blossomed into a full-fledged attorney. After a couple of years in the smaller office there, I moved across the hall and effectively doubled my leased space. The new office also had a conference room, which made mine a genuine law practice.

Mary Bhardwaj was an attorney and a stay-at-home mom. Mary had two girls; her daughter Kiran was Kane's age. I knew Mary from church. She came to work in my office and we dovetailed perfectly. Just when we were getting ourselves organized, however, Mary's husband got an out-of-state job offer and they moved away. When Mary left, I lost a trusted colleague, but she remains my close friend.

Mary has the distinction of being the *last* partner I had, and we are still good friends today. She comes back to Arkansas on occasion, and we always try to meet and catch up.

When she left, I did some soul-searching and finally decided I needed to *own* my office. After patient searching, I found a red brick house at 127 East Third Street and bought it. This transpired in 2000. My father helped me with the financing. The house had green and gold shag carpet and a pink bathroom. In fact, all the bathroom fixtures were pink—even the bathtub. When we refurbished the house, I turned the bathroom from pink to a more professional-looking white. The location was wonderful; I was directly across from the Pope County Library and the Russellville post office. At that time, about a quarter of all Russellville residents would come to the post office on a daily basis to collect their mail.

The red-brick house worked well for several years. Then, in 2006, opportunity knocked. I bought a two-story house located in the same block, which meant I was still directly across the street from the busy post office.

Built in 1908, just a couple of years after Russellville's devastating 1906 fire, the converted two-story residence on East Second Street was the office I'd always dreamed of having. There was a wrap-around columned porch, a dormer upstairs that held all my files, and even a sleeping porch. The office had been occupied by a local real estate agency, so it was computer-ready. All Bob and I needed to do was repaint the downstairs, and the new space was ready to go.

Since my old office and my new office were literally back to back, Bob's professor friends helped us carry boxes of files and furniture from one place to the other. Then I rented out the red brick house to a drug rehabilitation center, and gave them a big break on the rent. Suddenly, I was a landlady! I'd never intended to own property that I could rent. When I bought the new office, I had an enclosed office in a separate building as well. I rented that to a food pantry called Ray of Hope, and gave them a substantial break on the rent.

I eventually grew tired of being a landlady, and sold the red brick house in February, 2020. The Covid pandemic began a month or so later, so selling the real property when I did proved to be a commendable prudence.

The big old house into which I moved had light grey siding with cranberry shutters, and I quickly came to love the place. The vintage two-story was in good shape with no apparent mold or leakage. The beautiful leaded glass front door dated back to 1908, when the house was built. The wooden frame matched the rather austere pine trim in the house. The pine trim had been shipped up from New Orleans, so this made the house somewhat unique, especially for

Russellville. There were huge sliding pocket doors, a large kitchen with a range and dishwasher, a spacious conference room, big windows and abundant sunlight.

Upstairs, there were several offices, including a living room where I could take a nap in my recliner. Kane would come to the office after school. He'd watch DVDs and play video games on the television in another upstairs room.

My two-story office held within it the presence of people who had lived there over the decades. In the evenings, I'd be in town and go upstairs. The office was empty … at least, there were no other *people* there. I don't believe in ghosts, but I honestly felt the presence of the generations who had lived in the house during the years when it was a private residence.

I stayed in that office until I retired in the spring of 2020, and I kept it for several years after I stopped practicing. When Jim Moore moved back to Arkansas to be with me after Bob's death, he made one of the upstairs offices into a little writer's studio. I became accustomed to walking part way up the twisting staircase and listening as Jim keyboarded or talked on the phone. Jim has often said that of all the offices he's had during his career, that office in my big two-story was his favorite.

Over the years, the big old house became a second home for me. Clients would make an appointment or just walk in and tell me their legal and personal problems *ad nauseam.* I tried to get a word in edgewise when I could, just so I could get to the facts of the case. Those facts would help me advise them on how best to remedy their legal problem.

Sometimes, an obnoxious person would come in and complain about their current spouse, with whom they had two or three children. They told me more than I wanted to know about the abusive or alcoholic individual they'd married. Of course, it occurred to me that they should have figured out their spouse wasn't a good parent after the first baby! Some of the clients had just had a third or fourth baby with the awful spouse about whom they were complaining.

Since the spouse was also the legal parent of the children, it was often hard to cut the spouse completely out of the picture. I got my client custody, but the spouse would typically get visitation. I patiently explained that the spouse had parental rights unless there was a police report or actual evidence of abuse.

Of course, many clients did not want to hear this, and they became quite upset. They'd tell me they intended to find a 'good lawyer' who would keep the other parent away from the children. Usually, they'd storm out, slamming my heavy glass door as they left. I always breathed a sigh of relief when the door survived the client's wrath. In all my years of law practice, I had nary a front door broken! That's not something all attorneys can say.

The opposite type of client was a very depressed individual who would come in and tell me their sad story. Hearing that they'd waited too long—because of the Statute of Limitations or some other reason—wasn't what they expected, and many began to sob when I told them that I had no magic wand with which to solve their problems.

The real problem often became getting the sobbing client out of my office. After using a copious wad of Kleenex, most got up and left of their own accord.

I'd had my law office in the old house just over a year when the most defining tragedy of my life unfolded. As I walked out to my car one early February evening, there was a smell of snow in the air. About 30 minutes later, I pulled into my driveway at home and expected to see my son's Toyota parked there. Kane wasn't home, I quickly realized, but he should have gotten there hours ahead of me. Kane was 17, attending the Arkansas School for Math, Science, and the Arts in Hot Springs, about 100 miles south of where we lived. On this particular Thursday, he was coming home to enjoy the long President's Day weekend. Bob sat alone in the house, as mystified as I was.

I'd been home for about 30 minutes when a man appeared on our front deck. Since we lived in a heavily-wooded area in the foothills of the Ozark National Forest, visitors traipsing across our deck were something of a novelty. We opened the front door and greeted Rodney, who was the town Marshall in nearby Dover, Arkansas. Almost immediately, I knew Rodney wasn't paying us a social call.

Rodney's expression was quite grim. He said, "There's been an accident. Your son was in a bad car wreck coming up Highway 7 near Ola. He's in surgery now, at St. Vincent Infirmary in Little Rock."

I turned away from the door, and I remember that the entire living room started to spin in front of me. I sagged, but Bob caught me and held me upright. Kane was my baby, my only child, and the joy of my life. In a moment, I was shaking uncontrollably. Bob held me while I calmed down. One of us had to think rationally just then, and Bob could still do that. He asked Rodney what we should do.

Rodney looked at us and his eyes brimmed with tears of sympathy. "Why don't you pack things for the night and go to Little Rock to be with Kane," he said quietly. Of course, that's what Bob and I did. Snow was swirling down as we started the 100-mile drive to the Arkansas capitol.

Back then, in our area, cellphones were still something of a novelty, and we had no real news en route. When we arrived at the hospital, we learned that Kane had survived his surgery. Our son made it through the night. Bob and I went to a hotel in the early hours of the next morning, but we barely slept.

When we returned to the hospital, doctors told us that Kane was in a coma from which he would likely never awaken. Their scans showed that our son had no brain activity. That's the reason Kane's shattered pelvis had been left as it was; there was no real reason for the additional surgery. I looked out the hospital window and stared into the bright noonday sun. Although I didn't want to accept it, I knew instinctively that our death vigil had begun. Kane was mercifully oblivious, but Bob and I were in the deep rapids.

Those next ten days were the longest of my life. We let Kane slip away on Saturday, and Bob and I returned to our home. The sense of loss was both constant and profound; everywhere I turned in our house, there was something that reminded me of Kane.

My only consolation was that a part of Kane lived on. His donated organs helped a half-dozen people live new and fulfilling lives. Not long ago, I received a letter from the parents of a little girl who received one of Kane's kidneys. The enclosed photo showed the child dancing joyfully ... something that would likely not have been possible without Kane's sacrifice. My son, the parents told me, had been their daughter's saving angel.

Parents are not supposed to outlive their children. For my part, life had to go on. I did the only thing I could. I got up the next day, drove to Russellville and threw myself into my work. My stunned secretary could not believe I was at my desk. Work became my refuge, and the Monday grind was a solace of sorts. I remember I did a guardianship to rescue a young boy from his drug-addicted mother and father. I felt the usual satisfaction in a job well done, but there was no joy in the work. All the joy had been ripped from me. At Kane's memorial service that Thursday, I told myself that I could laugh again and smile again—at some point—but that I would never be truly happy again. That was a sad self-fulfilling prophecy, but it has largely been proven true. Even the happiness I experience today is still mingled with a sense of profound loss.

During the week following Kane's death, my thoughts turned back to when I was just 10 years old. Both of my grandfathers had died in the same summer. That 1966 experience taught me about peaks and valleys. When life is going well and you feel on top of the world, you are at the peak of the human experience. When something incredibly painful intrudes—as my son's death demonstrated—that event sends you deep into the valley.

Bob often told me, "Life goes on, Susan." For the next couple of years, I literally could not see how that was the case. A part of my heart died with Kane. For a year or more, I told myself that Kane had taken a space journey to Mars or that he was in a faraway land, unable to contact me. The sheer finality of my son's death was something I wanted to avoid at any cost.

I am a woman of faith, and I honestly believe that God will not give us more than we can handle. I asked God for the strength I'd need to continue to live and breathe, and I prayed for help as I began to climb out of the deep, desolate valley.

Other people I knew made an effort to offer support. A couple of weeks after Kane's death, I received a handwritten note from Richard Peel:

> *2/28/07*
> *Susan Allen;*
> *I cannot now, nor do I ever wish to feel the depths of your despair. Life, although not of all that we might want for, goes on. Jennifer, John and I offer whatever assistance you might require.*
> *A colleague and friend,*
> *Richard Peel*

Several months after Kane's death, I received a letter from Jim Moore. The envelope bore a British stamp. Jim had been living in London for the past several years. If I have ever questioned the often-incomprehensible love Jim bears for me, his letter put those qualms to rest.

> *Dear Susan;*
> *Words cannot express how shocked I was to learn of Kane's passing. I'm sure he was as energetic, intelligent and idealistic as you*

were when I knew you. You and Bob have suffered a loss that cannot be weighed.

I literally cannot imagine how you survived the past few months. I was not there to offer help in your most challenging time, and that fact saddens me. Perhaps I might have made some small difference … and I certainly would have tried.

Kane's death is a deep personal tragedy for me because he was your son. In my entire life, I have loved two women unconditionally: my mother, and you. When your mother was dying, I told you I would give my life to keep a life you loved beside you. I wish I could have made good on that promise; I would gladly trade all the things I've done for all the things Kane will never do.

Miles and years separate us, but you have never been far from my heart. Please accept my sympathy, best wishes and abiding love. I'm thinking of earlier times.

Always,
Jim

Bob was right: Life does go on. The high points are still there to be savored, but daily living is muddled a bit by the bitterness one finds in the deepest valleys of the human existence. I suppose it cannot be otherwise, but—like Jim—I'd give anything to have my son here again. Kane has now been dead longer than he was alive, but the vacant place in my heart stubbornly refuses to be filled.

CHAPTER TWELVE

Looking Forward, Looking Back

Britain's Queen Elizabeth I, arguing for the formation of the Church of England, called common sense "a most English virtue." Since I'm descended from Englishmen and Englishwomen, I must have inherited more common sense than most other lawyers.

And that's a good thing, because I always found law practice ethics to be simple common sense: Don't gossip, don't represent both sides, and don't steal other people's money. There are numerous canons of ethics. You'd be amazed how many attorneys manage to muck them up!

I tried my best to be an honest lawyer. Bob's mother even needlepointed me an 'Honest Lawyer' sign. I hung that sign in my office as a matter of pride; I did not bribe judges or witnesses in cases, I declared my cash income, and I tried my best to be honest in every way possible.

In law school, we actually had an ethics class to teach us how to practice law within specific ethical boundaries. Once I had finished the class, I then had to pass a multi-state ethics exam. This ethics exam was in addition to the three-day bar exam I took after I finished law school.

At some point when I was in practice, I discovered that I had a singular lack of appreciation for lawyer jokes. People like to quote Shakespeare, who said, "First thing we do, let's kill all the lawyers." The American public tends to believe that all lawyers are crooked and greedy. However, when someone is in real trouble, they typically *want* to find the meanest, crookedest attorney they can find! A bare-knuckled litigator, I've learned, is something akin to a junkyard dog. No one wants to pick a fight with such an attorney, and they're not usually held up as a model of virtue and propriety.

The bottom line is sad but true: People don't want an honest attorney. Instead, they want an attorney who will win their case! An ethical solicitor, which is the British equivalent of a lawyer, is a genuine rarity ... something akin to an honest man in Parliament. This shows you that the Brits share our attitude toward attorneys and politicians!

Once I began practicing law, it became pretty evident that many other lawyers had chosen to forget their ethics training. For some of my colleagues, the ethics grounding they'd received in law school seemed irretrievably lost, like something that was blown away in a sort of giant cosmic slipstream.

One of the most important canons of ethics is to avoid a conflict of interest. One codicil of the Arkansas Rules of Professional Conduct—1.7—deals with conflicts of interest when representing clients. If, for example, a wife came into my office to consult with me about a divorce, and then her husband subsequently made an appointment to discuss the divorce, I'd have a conflict of interest if I took the appointment and met with the husband.

An attorney may only represent one side in any case. This always seemed simple and inordinately logical to me, but some attorneys had difficulty following this commonsense approach. Bill Smith, another local lawyer, had filed a divorce for the wife. However, the parties never actually got divorced, and the case remained open in the courthouse files. Once the parties had reconciled, the case needed to be dismissed. Mr. Smith just left it hanging, perhaps in the forlorn hope that love would not triumph and the wife would require his services yet again.

Well, the wife came to see me, wanting the divorce after all. She explained that she'd hired Mr Smith, who had never finalized the divorce. My new client wanted her divorce finalized forthwith.

I went to the courthouse to look at the file, and found that Mr. Smith's name was indeed on the case as the attorney of record. I filed a motion to dismiss the old divorce, then filed the new divorce case for the wife. Mr. Smith flabbergasted me by answering the complaint on behalf of the *husband*, which meant he was effectively representing both parties in the same divorce process.

Clearly, Mr. Smith saw no problem with that course of action. I did.

As politely as I could, I requested that Mr. Smith withdraw as the husband's attorney. I thought his recusal was only common sense, and I was a bit surprised when Mr. Smith refused. When we appeared at an open divorce hearing, the central issue was Mr. Smith's rather evident conflict of interest. Mr. Smith actually tried to argue with the judge that this sort of lawyerly conduct was allowed under the rules. The judge was apparently as unimpressed as I; Mr. Smith lost. The judge ruled that Mr. Smith had a conflict of interest and was required to withdraw as attorney for the husband. From a commonsense standpoint, of course, this particular outcome was never in much doubt. Law is common sense, but for some attorneys, the two seem never to intersect.

Money management in a law office is another commonsense area where specific requirements apply. Pursuant to Rule 1.15 of the Arkansas Rules of Professional Conduct, the attorney must "safekeep" property and have a trust account. The attorney is supposed to hold the property of clients or third parties—including prospective clients—in the trust account, and keep that money separate from the lawyer's own funds. In fact, a lawyer can be disbarred for wrongfully taking money from the trust account.

This process is designed to work in a certain way, and as long as it isn't violated, it typically does. For example, when a client paid me a retainer, the money had to go into my trust account. I would withdraw a portion of the money as I earned it via filings or billable hours. But an attorney cannot 'borrow' money from their trust account. If an attorney settles an accident case, for example, all the proceeds from the settlement are put into the trust account until it can be divided between the client, attorney and payment of medical bills and other legitimate expenses.

Rules 1.15 and 1.17 are easy enough to understand. But Rule 1.26 of the Arkansas Rules of Professional Conduct is a little more complex. This Rule focuses on the confidentiality of client information. Much like a priest in a confessional, every lawyer has an ethical obligation to hold *inviolate* the confidential information of the client.

Whatever information the client confides, the attorney cannot divulge it for any reason. For example, I couldn't talk with my husband about my client's case unless I'd filed the case in open court and the filing was thereby public knowledge. While the facts in the complaint or petition are a matter of public record, the attorney-client exchange is privileged information.

Rule 1.26 is essentially the reason that, in a divorce action, an attorney can only represent one side. The lawyer would effectively betray one client by sharing the confidential information one spouse had confided with the other spouse.

The pressure to win every case causes inordinate stress, both for the attorney and the client. I think I've watched every Perry Mason episode in which Raymond Burr starred, and I'll be darned if I can find one instance in which Perry Mason appears to be under a good deal of stress. Most of the time, Perry appears to be under no stress at all! If Erle Stanley Gardner ever recorded an instance of Perry Mason—or Della Street, his assistant—needing to imbibe Alka-Seltzer, I have never found it.

From my first days of practice to my retirement, I found the stress of being an attorney both real and palpable. When our national discourse took a hard right turn in the summer of 2016, I was suddenly confronted by clients who were just downright rude. The politics of the time—the end of the Obama era and the beginning of the Trump presidency—seemed to embolden many clients to the point of pugnacity and beyond.

By the summer of 2017, I was realizing that while I still enjoyed practicing law, I didn't enjoy dealing with a few of my clients and some of the other local attorneys. What should have been a pleasant, friendly exchange had become sharper, more pointed and more accusatory. This was particularly noticeable in conservative Pope County. Clients appeared to be just plain angry with Ashlee and me, and many seemed to feel that every mess in their lives was somehow my fault.

I think that was the point at which I began to consider what my life might be like without the daily grind of a law practice. Just as there is no real status quo in daily life, however, there seems to be no after-practice life for most lawyers. Over the years, I had become convinced that good lawyers didn't retire … they just wither away and die.

I remember a 78-year-old male colleague of mine proclaimed that he would never retire. "They'll just have to take my body out of my office when that time comes," he told me. I would ask other older attorneys when *they* were going to retire. "Retire?" they exclaimed. "What would I do all day? I practice law; there's nothing else I would want to do with my time."

Well, I—for one—had other things to do with *my* time. I was determined to change the no-retirement paradigm. I had no intention of dying at my desk. By that point, I guess, I was no longer enjoying my practice as I should have … my office and staff were a means to an end. I still enjoyed serving others, but the effort was taking a mighty toll on me.

My husband, Bob, had retired as a professor of organic chemistry at age 65. People would ask him if he ever became bored. "No," he'd respond cheerfully, "every day is a Saturday!" That was an easy thing for Bob to say; he was a confirmed Atheist. I began to suspect that my male colleagues - the ones who didn't want to retire - just didn't want to be at home with their wives all day!

Of course, the easy solution to the retirement conundrum or problem is to volunteer at your church or a local school, exercise each day, take up a hobby like golf, tennis or pickleball, and go to exotic places, like Australia or South America.

As I look back, I realize that I enjoyed practicing law because I enjoyed working with other attorneys. Several of my male colleagues, like Doc Irwin, Dale Finley, David Eddy and Ken Hodges, were happy to pitch in and help when I was stuck on a case and didn't know how to proceed. I'm not sure there are many industries in which competitors help each other, and I've always been grateful for the help I've had over the years.

I enjoyed serving my clients as well. Like my attorney friends, I became quite close to several of our office clients. Two of my favorite clients were John and Ellen. They had a son, John, Jr., a daughter-in-law, and a young grandchild. After my son Kane died, John and Ellen came to my office for help. A tornado in nearby Atkins, Arkansas, had killed the son, his wife and their little granddaughter. Since I'd lost a child, my heart went out to them.

Ashlee and I genuinely enjoyed having John and Ellen came by to visit. This unique couple brought cheer to the office ... they reminded me that I had not lost a daughter-in-law and a grandchild as they had. Since neither Ellen nor John had any brothers or sisters, they had no heirs. Theirs was one of the saddest estate cases I had.

My best friend in high school and college went to law school just as I did, but she went to an east coast school while I headed west. We both wound up practicing law in Arkansas, but her area of specialty is far removed from mine. She is 68 now, as I am as I write this chapter, and my friend has no desire to retire.

"Do you want to be found dead at your desk?" I finally asked her. I, for one, had other ideas. My husband was always sharing the joys of retirement and I wanted to experience at least some of them for myself.

So, in early 2018, I began thinking through the process of shutting down my law office. In my particular business, this was a challenge. I'd often complete a divorce when the client's children were very small, and one party or the other would be back to follow up on issues affecting visitation and child support. Each case I took represented a never-ending cycle.

Closing my office took two full years. The 24-month rundown ended in early 2020. I wrapped up my practice just prior to the onset of the Covid-19 pandemic. As you might imagine, the 2019 holiday season and the early weeks of 2020 were a slow time! Ashlee and I would talk and laugh when things were quiet. We'd even play music and dance in her office. The one client who caught us actually joined in.

Retiring was not always a purely analytical process. When I told clients I was going to retire, several cried and told me I could not. I told them I'd make sure to find them another attorney who would treat them well. I had just finished my last hearing when the Covid pandemic hit in 2020. At that point, social distancing rules meant that lawyers could not go to court or have their clients come talk to them. As I drove through Russellville, I saw other lawyers meeting with clients beneath tents or awnings outside their offices! I was so glad I didn't have to manage the logistics of practicing law during the pandemic.

If life is a journey, then retirement is a pretty significant step. In those first few weeks after I'd closed my practice, I often woke up not knowing the day of the week. I'd fill my hours playing fetch with my dogs, tending my sheep, reading, taking nature walks and playing the piano.

My retirement wasn't exactly a bed of roses, however. Bob was entering the final stage of his long battle with cancer. He had developed bladder cancer and the disease had spread; as 2020 wore on, he needed my help more and more often. For more than a year, my other part-time job was as a home health aide. That work was far more grueling than law practice had been! Bob's cancer had metastasized to his lungs, brain and spine. Although we tried not to focus on it, we knew the sand was running out of the hourglass.

In many ways, Bob's death in 2021 was the impetus I needed to begin outlining this book. Like a clock spring that had been wound too tight, I felt a sudden, almost bewildering absence of worry, stress and tension. The new-found freedom unleashed a torrent of creative energy, and it was up to me to direct that energy in the most productive ways I could.

After Bob died, I began trying to expand my creativity in a number of ways. I found drawing lessons on YouTube and started sketching. I worked to improve my watercolor skill. If Grandma Moses could paint beautiful primitives at age 90, I'd decided, then I could become an artist in my 60s. I found that I still loved to create. I was able to give free rein to my artistic tendencies, and my comparative lack of skill was just another problem to be solved.

My mother always told me that "You're only bored if you want to be. Use that brain of yours and create something fun to do." So I had no fear of retiring, and I've loved it so far. Except for Sundays, when I go to church, every day *is* a Saturday!

Even on Saturdays, however, there's much to do. Life in the 100-acre woods seems inexorably busy; I'm up and walking in the early morning, spend part of the early hours drawing, painting or writing, and often settle down with the dogs for a little television in the early afternoons. The house Bob and I built is filled with large plate-glass windows, and I can watch the sun move through a slow east-to-west arc as each day wears on.

Sometimes, in the late afternoons usually, my mind wanders back thirty years or more, to a time when everyone I loved was still alive. I think about Bob and Kane, about my mother and father. The memories are a refuge of sorts, and some are so vivid that I have to brush them away like flies.

I see myself practicing at the piano while my long-suffering mother cooks dinner.

I see myself as an eighth-grader, sitting in Doc Irwin's Sunday School class.

I see my father giving me one of his pedantic lectures in response to a question I've asked about something in his area of expertise—history or political science.

I see myself as a VISTA volunteer, walking a neighborhood street in West Dallas.

I see Bob floating down the Buffalo River with a raft full of wide-eyed students.

I see Kane as a precocious four-year-old, telling me he knew more than I did.

I see Ashlee sitting at her desk, holding my puppy Lenny in her arms.

For a few moments, at least, I'm once again that idealistic young woman who headed off to Dallas and law school, intent on changing the world. Being called to serve, I've discovered, is something like having a double-edged sword dangling above you. If you do too much, you stand to lose a good deal of your own soul. If you do too little, on the other hand, you have to live with the knowledge that you did not do all you could.

In many ways, the journey is its own reward. As I watched Perry Mason years ago, I imagined my law career would be dominated by high courtroom drama. That Hollywood invention never even makes the list of things I think about today. I'm glad I was called to help more than 3,000 clients at times in their lives when they *needed* the help. Helping others never really made me healthier, wealthier or even exceptionally wise, but in the final accounting, I'm hard-pressed to imagine that my efforts will have been found wanting.

My parents, Kenneth and Marylou Walker, about 1950.

A studio photo from late 1958. I was two years old.

On the Arkansas Tech campus in 1961.

Dad with his first book,
The Days the Presidents Died,
in 1966.

Above: I am helping my cousin's two boys read at Christmas 1974.

Left: After graduation from law school, I waited for California Bar exam results at my parents' house.

'Money means nothing', so she joins VISTA

A Russellville native elected as the girl most likely to succeed in her senior year at Arkansas Tech has realized that "money means nothing" to her and has joined VISTA (Volunteer in Service to America) in Dallas, Texas.

"Sure, I like money," said Susan Walker, 21, "but it couldn't make me happy. I don't value material things. I'm joining VISTA because it's the thing that could be done for no monetary gain."

Miss Walker is the daughter of Dr. and Mrs. Kenneth Walker of Russellville. She has a bachelor's degree in science and elementary education, and plays violin and piano.

She has recently completed four days of intensive training in Dallas and begun working as a community organizer with the Block Partnership in Dallas.

"It's the best thing I can do with my life," Miss Walker said.

She said she had thought about the Peace Corps, but decided on VISTA "because there are a lot of conflicts in the world and some Peace Corps countries are unstable. This is my first time away from home. VISTA is challenging enough."

The Block Partnership VISTAs go into communities and talk to residents about their problems. Once the community has come up with the priorities, the volunteers get the residents in contact with a local church group. They sign a six-month contract and become the block (street) partners.

The Block Partnership concept was brought in from St. Louis by a former Dallas mayor in 1968. The program is sponsored by the Greater Dallas Council of Churches and currently numbers 11 VISTAs.

While in Texas, Miss Walker will live on a monthly allowance of about $255.

Some 4,700 VISTAs, budgeted at $25 million, work at 800 projects nationwide. Almost 90 of them serve in Arkansas. VISTAs, as well as 6,700 Peace Corps volunteers in 64 developing nations, are part of the federal volunteer agency ACTION.

An average VISTA contributes about $9,865 in antipoverty services a year, according to a recent ACTION study. It costs almost $5,460 to place a volunteer in the field, meaning that VISTA's average worth is 181 percent of his or her cost.

Persons interested in joining VISTA or the Peace Corps may call collect the recruiting office in Dallas at (214) 749-1855, ext. 23.

VISTA VOLUNTEER — Susan Walker, 21, daughter of Dr. and Mrs. Kenneth Walker of Russellville has recently joined VISTA (Volunteer in Service to America) in Dallas, Texas.

Our local newspaper told the story after I departed for VISTA in July, 1978.

Jim Moore took this photo of me at the Spruce Goose in Long Beach in the summer of 1983. I'd not yet taken the California Bar exam.

With my aunt Jane outside my office in early 1985.

An office of my own! I stayed in this little red-brick house for about 6 years.

Bob and I cutting the cake at our wedding reception.
The date was May 19, 1985; we were married nearly 36 years.

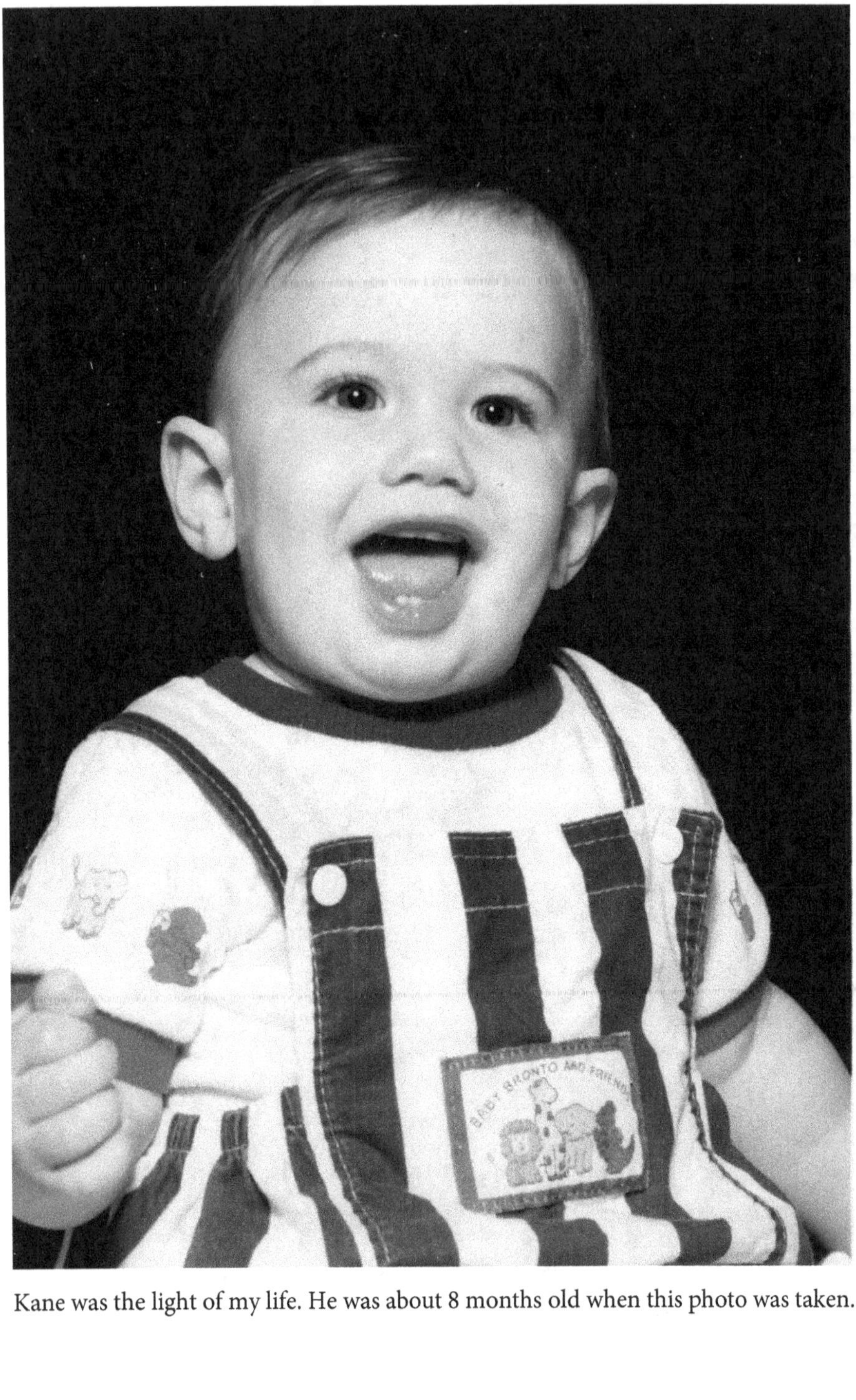

Kane was the light of my life. He was about 8 months old when this photo was taken.

Helping Kane learn to canoe. He was about 4 years old.

With Bob and Kane in Hawaii.

When I moved into my big two-story office in 2006, I made sure the whole town knew.

One of my favorite photos with Kane, about 1997.

Speaking as a candidate for Municipal Judge, about a year after Kane's death.

www.ingramcontent.com/pod-product-compliance
Lightning Source LLC
LaVergne TN
LVHW052326200926
848481LV00002B/684

* 9 7 9 8 2 1 8 8 1 7 8 3 1 *